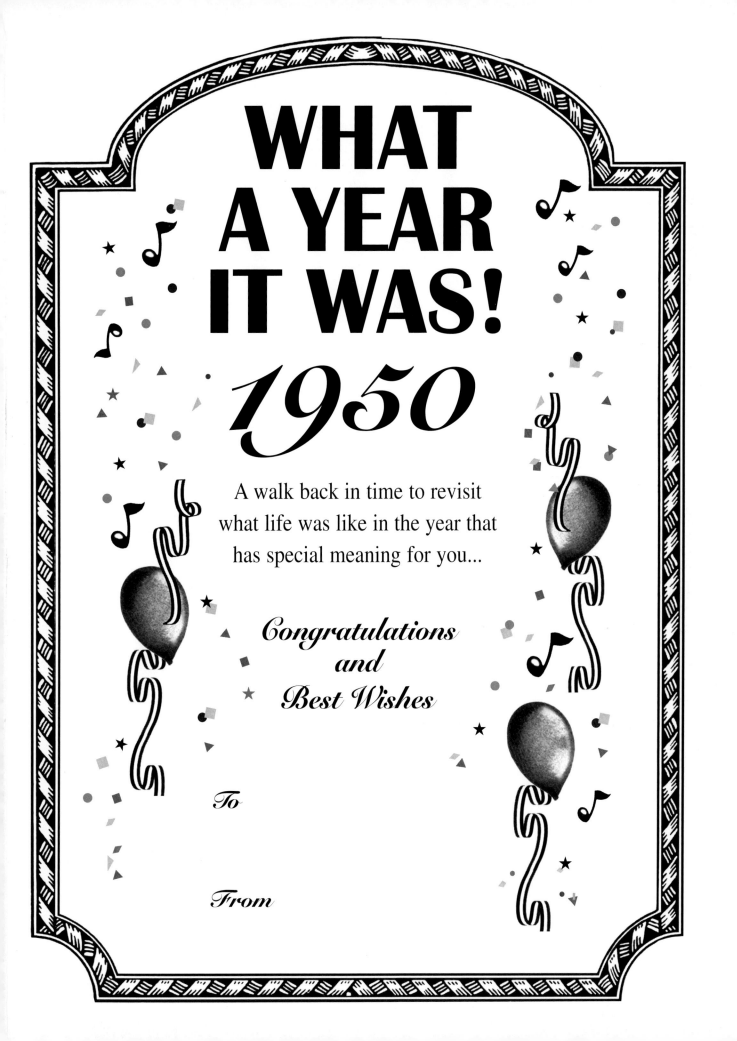

WHAT A YEAR IT WAS!

1950

A walk back in time to revisit
what life was like in the year that
has special meaning for you...

*Congratulations
and
Best Wishes*

To

From

DEDICATION

To Derrell...
You Are Living Proof That
We Walk Among The Angels
Happy 50th Birthday

Designers • Peter Hess & Marguerite Jones
Research and Special Segments Writer • Laurie Cohn

CONTENTS

POLITICS and WORLD EVENTS

President Truman's Press Conference

"The cause of freedom is being challenged throughout the world today by the forces of imperialistic Communism. This is a struggle above all else for the mind of man...We must make ourselves heard 'round the world in our great campaign of truth..."

Headline: The Korean Crisis

300,000 Chinese Communist Troops Cross The Manchurian Border Into Korea

Top defense officials gather at the White House to discuss the gravest world crisis since Poland and Pearl Harbor.

Secretary of State Dean Acheson arrives to discuss the unexpected entry of Red Chinese troops into Korea which could precipitate World War III.

President Truman voices his accusation of Red imperialism:

"The forces of the United Nations are in Korea to put down an aggression that threatens not only the whole fabric of the United Nations but all human hopes of peace and justice... If aggression is successful in Korea, we can expect it to spread throughout Asia and Europe and to this hemisphere. We are fighting in Korea for our own national security and survival. We have committed ourselves to the cause of a just and peaceful world order... We stand by that commitment."

WHAT A YEAR IT WAS!

On The Korean Battlefront

United Nations Forces Fight Desperately To Meet The Red Attack

Our troops must face what General MacArthur terms "a new war."

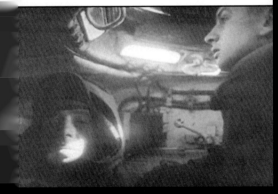

Outnumbered more than two to one by Chinese and North Koreans, the U.N. forces hope to regroup and to meet the overwhelming attack which has broken their lines of defense across North Korea.

President Truman states that the use of the atomic bomb is being considered to halt the Russian-inspired Communist expansion.

UNITED NATIONS MEETS AT LAKE SUCCESS TO DISCUSS THE GRAVE KOREAN CRISIS

The Red Chinese delegation from Peking hear themselves charged with each of their crimes by the representative of the Republic of Korea, Ben See Lim:

"I point my finger at these representatives of the Chinese Communist regime and I ask why do they come here with unclean hands? I ask again, why does this group come here with the hands that drip with the blood, the blood of the United Nations troops, the blood of the Korean people?"

The Chinese delegation refuses to take their seats and face their accuser.

NEW B.F. Goodrich

"RYTHM RIDE"

GIVES YOU MORE COMFORT

GREATER SAFETY — LONGER MILEAGE

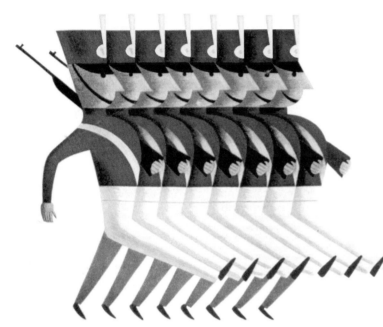

1 Like the awkward squad above, most tire cords work *out of rythm*. They're loosely tied by cross threads that carry no load, and interfere with cord action. The shackled cords bunch or gap, strain too hard or loaf.

2 There are NO CROSS THREADS in B. F. Goodrich tire cords. BFG cords work *in rythm* like marchers at left. They carry impact from one to another. All flex *together* to resist road shock for more blow-out protection . . . cushion bumps for more comfort . . . share wear for more mileage . . . give you "Rythm Ride"!

IF YOU CAN TELL WHICH MARCHERS ARE BEST, YOU CAN TELL WHICH TIRE IS BEST!

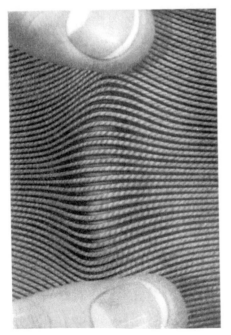

3 With old-type cords (left), weak spots invite trouble, overstrained cords wear out too soon, uneven action makes for an uneven ride.

4 Photo (left) shows how BFG "rythmic-flexing cords" are sealed in rubber with no cross threads, perfectly spaced, under uniform tension. No slacker cords. No overstrained cords. Every cord shares the load equally.

5 See the big difference in tires at your B. F. Goodrich dealer's—right inside the tire. B. F. Goodrich alone has the equipment and skills to give you "rythmic-flexing cords" in every tire for every purpose! Buy now! Small down-payment. Convenient terms. The B. F. Goodrich Company, Akron, Ohio.

RESEARCH KEEPS **B.F.Goodrich** FIRST IN RUBBER

9

1950

United Nations Forces Dig In For A Winter's Stand Against Overwhelming Red Chinese Hordes

Accompanied by General Walton Walker, General MacArthur, Commander-In-Chief in the Far East, visits the fighting front in Korea, his first since the Chinese attack drew the alliance back from the Manchurian border.

Following his inspection trip, the General expresses confidence that his forces will be able to hold their own.

WHAT A YEAR IT WAS!

Acheson Makes Peace Plea Before The United Nations General Assembly

"The peace the world wants must be free from fear— the fear of invasion, the fear of subversion, the fear of the knock on the door at midnight. The peace the world wants must be free from want— the peace in which neighbors help each other and together build a better life. The peace the world wants must be a moral peace so that the spirit of man may be free and the barriers between the hearts and minds of men may drop away and leave men free to unite in brotherhood. This is the task before us."

President Truman welcomes Prime Minister Attlee as he arrives in Washington for a series of talks with the chief executive. The two heads of state will attempt to arrive at a solution in the struggle against Communism.

England's Prime Minister Attlee In U.S. As Chinese Reds Force Allies Back

The threat to Europe as well as the Far East will form the basis of their discussions and Mr. Attlee makes a brief statement:

"Prime in these talks is to align our policies in the new and troubled situation in the world and to find the means of upholding what we both know to be right."

KOREA

JUNE

North Korean Communist Forces Cross The 38th Parallel As They Launch A Full-Scale Attack Against South Korea — U.N. Security Council Orders A Cease-Fire And Immediate Withdrawal Of North Korean Troops.

Tanks Begin Invasion Of Seoul, Capital Of Republic Of Korea.

President Truman Orders U.S. Naval And Air Force Support For South Korea And U.S. 7th Fleet To Protect Formosa.

As Seoul Falls To The North, General MacArthur Flies To South Korea To Oversee The Situation.

JULY

U.S. Forces Face Action In Korea — Are Successful In First Significant Engagement.

American Tank Divisions Go Into Combat.

Australia, Great Britain And New Zealand Commit Regiments To Korea Under The Auspices Of The United Nations.

SEPTEMBER

With A Daring Surprise Beach Landing At Inchon, U.N. Forces Go On The Offensive.

U.S. Marines In Seoul.

Seoul Is Regained By U.N. Soldiers Several Months After Being Taken Over by Chinese Troops — Acting On Behalf Of The U.N., General MacArthur Hands Back The Capital To President Syngman Rhee Of The Republic Of Korea.

OCTOBER

Supported By World Opinion But Denounced By Communist China, U.S. Armed Forces Cross The 38th Parallel.

United Nations Regiments Arrive At The Chinese-Korean Border.

General MacArthur Urges North Korea To Surrender.

NOVEMBER

In An Effort To End The Korean War By Christmas, 100,000 U.N. Troops Begin Assault. 200,000 Red Troops Launch Offensive Against U.N. Forces.

● **PYONGYANG**

38th Parallel

● **SEOUL**

● **Inchon**

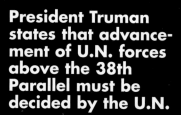

President Truman states that advancement of U.N. forces above the 38th Parallel must be decided by the U.N.

Chou En-lai threatens counter-attack if North Korea is invaded.

U.N. General Assembly passes resolution approving crossing 38th Parallel into North Korea by U.N. troops.

WHAT A YEAR IT WAS!

MacArthur

★ **In Accordance With U.N. Resolution, President Truman Appoints General Douglas MacArthur Commander-In-Chief Of All U.N. Forces In Korea.**

★ **General MacArthur's Use Of Ground Forces And Air Force Strikes Against Targets In North Korea Authorized By President Truman.**

★ **President Truman And General MacArthur Meet On Wake Island To Discuss The Korean War.**

★ **U.S. Asks Chiang Kai-shek To Confer With General MacArthur Before Committing 33,000 Troops To South Korea.**

U.N. Security Council calls for member nations to aid South Korea in resisting North Korean invasion.

Responding to the U.S. blockade of Korea, in a note sent to Washington the Soviet government accuses the U.S. of a new act of aggression and holds the U.S. accountable for damage to any Soviet interests.

Congress receives request from President Truman for $10 billion budget for arms.

Body Of Soviet Pilot Discovered In Plane U.S. Shoots Down Over Korea.

THE DRAFT

- Truman Says "U.S. Is Not At War" — Extends Draft Into 1951.

- President Truman Authorizes Beefing Up All U.S. Forces To Meet The Demands Of The Korean Situation Including Use Of Selective Service.

- U.S. Army Calls Up 62,000 National Guards And Enlisted Reservists To Active Duty For 21 Months And 100,000 Via Selective Service.

THE FACE OF COMMUNISM

BERLIN, powder keg of Europe, sees a mass demonstration of indoctrinated young Germans on May Day.

FRANCE is also beset by Communist-inspired strikes.

Red union members adopt violent methods to prevent the unloading of food and medicine sent under the Marshall Plan.

WHAT A YEAR IT WAS!

AROUND THE WORLD

In **JAPAN,** America's stronghold in the Pacific, the Communists create turmoil.

Students go on a rampage in Tokyo but are thwarted by Japanese police aided by occupation military.

In **AMERICA,** Union Square in New York is the back-drop for Red-instigated violence.

Should we face World War III, it is feared that saboteurs, spies and subversives will come from their ranks.

A Communist demonstrator is put into a police van.

Underlying the menace from within, Soviet Consul Valentin Gubitchev is deported after being convicted of receiving secret documents from government employee, Judith Coplon, who is also found guilty of spying.

CRISIS IN CHINA

The Red tide engulfing China washes on to yet another frontier. A border town in French Indochina peers across a narrow river at the silent menace of the Chinese Communist flag.

This French colony, itself beset by Red revolt, braces for invasion from the north where Communist victory on China's mainland is virtually a matter of history.

The seige of Southeast Asia is on as junks bearing starving Nationalist troops seek the only haven possible.

These demoralized troops of Chiang Kai-shek head for internment and disarmament in neutral French territory.

Asia is the gigantic pawn in global conflict as 150 men, a pathetic segment of Chiang Kai-shek's once mighty army, give up the struggle. Men who once fought the Japanese invader to a standstill succumb to their own fifth column.

In their wake, stream the bewildered casualties of civil war who instinctively seek freedom.

As the Red star rises over unconquerable China, freedom is the theme of **Madame Chiang Kai-shek's** plea as she prepares to join her husband on the island of Formosa, where he's established his refugee government:

"...It is with heavy heart that I note that a former ally, Britain, which sacrificed millions of lives on the altar of freedom, has now been taken by its leaders into the wilderness of political intrigue. Britain has bowed to the soul of a nation for a few pieces of silver... Russia will never know one day of peace in China, Russia will never own China, China will remain free..."

WHAT A YEAR IT WAS!

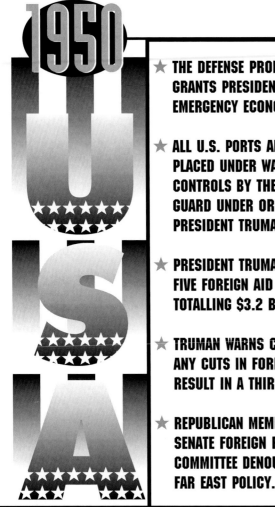

1950

U.S.A

★ THE DEFENSE PRODUCTION ACT GRANTS PRESIDENT TRUMAN EMERGENCY ECONOMIC POWERS.

★ ALL U.S. PORTS AND SHIPPING PLACED UNDER WARTIME CONTROLS BY THE U.S. COAST GUARD UNDER ORDERS FROM PRESIDENT TRUMAN.

★ PRESIDENT TRUMAN APPROVES FIVE FOREIGN AID PROGRAMS TOTALLING $3.2 BILLION.

★ TRUMAN WARNS CONGRESS THAT ANY CUTS IN FOREIGN AID COULD RESULT IN A THIRD WORLD WAR.

★ REPUBLICAN MEMBERS OF THE SENATE FOREIGN RELATIONS COMMITTEE DENOUNCE TRUMAN'S FAR EAST POLICY.

According To President Truman's Council Of Economic Advisers, The U.S. Has Reached Its Highest Prosperity In History.

Puerto Rican Assassins Mortally Wound A Guard Outside Blair House, President Truman's Temporary Residence, But Don't Get Near The President.

SECRETARY OF STATE DEAN ACHESON VOICES AMERICA'S IRREVOCABLE "HANDS-OFF" POLICY IN THE DEFENSE OF FORMOSA

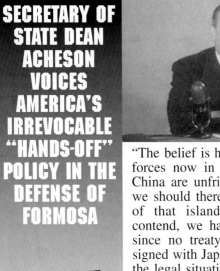

Secretary Of State Dean Acheson Calls For Seven-Point Cooperation Plan With Russia.

"The belief is held by some that the forces now in control of mainland China are unfriendly to us and that we should therefore prevent the fall of that island. Technically, they contend, we have a right to do so since no treaty of peace has been signed with Japan. Whatever may be the legal situation, the United States of America is not going to quibble about the integrity of its position. As the President states, we are not going to use our forces in connection with the present situation in Formosa. We are not going to attempt to seize the island. We are not going to get involved militarily in any way..."

★ U.S. On The Brink Of A Full-Fledged War With Chinese Communists.

★ U.S. Freezes All Chinese Funds Held In U.S. Territory And Bars U.S. Ships From Chinese Communist Ports.

To retaliate against Soviet transport restrictions in Germany, U.S. threatens new Berlin Airlift.

Stating that the United States must be "able to defend itself against any possible aggressor," President Truman orders hydrogen bomb built by the Atomic Energy Commission.

WHAT A YEAR IT WAS!

Joseph R. McCarthy, an unimportant, unpopular senator from Wisconsin, gains national spotlight as he begins his baseless anti-Red crusade by announcing to a women's club in Wheeling, West Virginia that Communists have infiltrated the State Department.

Senator Joseph McCarthy

McCarthy claims government official Owen Lattimore is a Russian agent.

President Truman strongly accuses McCarthy of trying to destroy American procedures abroad.

Senator McCarthy accused of making erroneous and reckless declarations by American diplomat Philip C. Jessup who claims McCarthy is endangering U.S. foreign relations.

★ FBI director **J. Edgar Hoover** and Attorney General **J. Howard McGrath** refuse Senate's request for files on State Department employees accused of disloyalty.

★ According to the chairman of the Loyalty Review Board, **Seth W. Richardson**, not one case of espionage in the U.S. Government has been uncovered.

★ The U.S. Supreme Court refuses to review the contempt convictions of two screenwriters thereby upholding the right of a congressional committee to force witnesses to disclose whether or not they are Communists.

CLAIMING HE DID NOT GIVE TOP SECRET DOCUMENTS TO FORMER COMMUNIST AGENT WHITTAKER CHAMBERS, ALGER HISS IS GIVEN A FIVE YEAR PRISON SENTENCE FOR PERJURY. A PSYCHIATRIST LABELS CHAMBERS A PSYCHOPATH DURING THE HISS TRIAL.

Alger Hiss

WHAT A YEAR IT WAS!

According to the Soviet Union all 1,939,163 German prisoners of war have been freed — West Germany challenges that number.

The U.S.S.R. reinstates death penalty for treason, espionage and sabotage.

Crew killed as Soviets shoot down American Navy plane flying over Latvia.

In the world's first jet-against-jet conflict, a Russian built MiG-15 is shot down over Korea by an American F-80 fighter jet.

Following two months of laborious discussions, Russia's **Joseph Stalin** and China's **Mao Tse-tung** sign a 30-year mutual defense treaty announcing to the world they are allies who will combine forces if necessary.

It is estimated that Russia has more combat planes, tanks and armed forces than the United States.

"Only National
has **all 4**
time-saving features
on **one** machine!"

"Complete Visibility at all times. I see all my postings at a glance, whether the carriage is open or closed. This saves time.

"Changes Posting Jobs in Seconds. Saves time. I switch control bars in seconds—changing posting jobs without moving from my chair."

"Full Amount Keyboard fills in all ciphers automatically. I operate two or more keys at once ... amounts are visible before printing—all this saves time, reduces errors."

"Electric Typewriter Keyboard. It's faster, smoother, easier. I can type description whenever desired. I get sharp, uniform multiple copies, too."

This NEW NATIONAL 31 also has many NEW AUTOMATIC FEATURES that cut costs. OVER 70 FUNCTIONS controlled automatically by arrangement of posting bars. SIMULTANEOUSLY ADDS and SUBTRACTS — or transfers balances — into any combination of totals. ENOUGH TOTALS for your needs. FLUID-DRIVE CARRIAGE—faster, smoother. Handles all accounting jobs. Call the National office today! See how this unprecedented combination of advantages will cut *your* accounting costs.

THE NATIONAL CASH REGISTER COMPANY
DAYTON 9, OHIO

National
ACCOUNTING MACHINES
CASH REGISTERS • ADDING MACHINES

21

Tribhuvana Bir Bikram Jung Bahadur Dethroned As Nepal's King.

Nepal's King Tribhuvana Bir Bikram Escapes Palace For Asylum In The Indian Embassy.

SOUTH AFRICA

Representing A Small Fraction Of The Populace, South Africa's White Assembly Votes To Separate The Country Into Sections According To Color.

Protesting Apartheid, Riots Break Out In Johannesburg.

South African Communist Party Is Dissolved.

Following violent clashes between Hindus and Moslems, INDIAN PRIME MINISTER JAWAHARLAL NEHRU and PAKISTANI PRIME MINISTER ALI KHAN sign a bill of rights for minorities.

Nehru

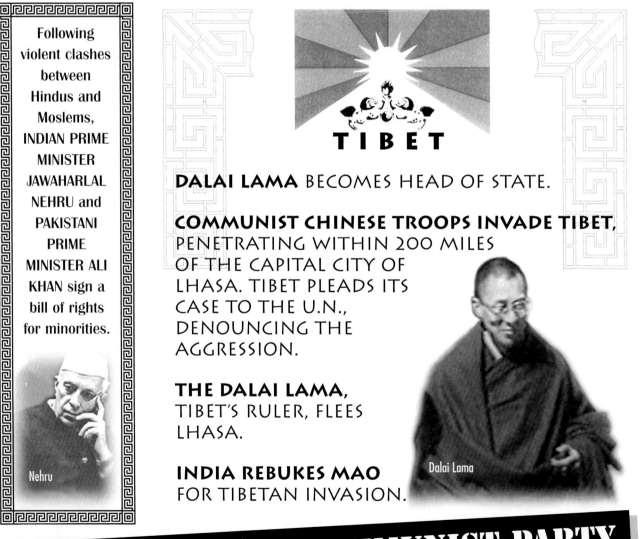

TIBET

DALAI LAMA BECOMES HEAD OF STATE.

COMMUNIST CHINESE TROOPS INVADE TIBET, PENETRATING WITHIN 200 MILES OF THE CAPITAL CITY OF LHASA. TIBET PLEADS ITS CASE TO THE U.N., DENOUNCING THE AGGRESSION.

THE DALAI LAMA, TIBET'S RULER, FLEES LHASA.

INDIA REBUKES MAO FOR TIBETAN INVASION.

Dalai Lama

AUSTRALIA BANS COMMUNIST PARTY

WHAT A YEAR IT WAS!

Middle East

Great Britain *Officially Recognizes Israel.*

Israel Announces *Jerusalem Is Now The Country's Capital.*

In A Dispute *With Conservative Cabinet Members, Israel's Premier David Ben-Gurion Resigns.*

David Ben-Gurion

Transjordan *Chooses New Name — Jordan.*

Mutual Defense Treaty *Signed By Arab League In Cairo.*

Winston Churchill's resolution for formation of a united European army to defend Western Europe is adopted by the Consultative Assembly of the Council of Europe.

Truman announces start of NATO as eight Western European nations sign pact.

NATO ministers meeting in The Hague approve plan to counter Soviet aggression.

VIETNAM...VIETNAM...VIETNAM...VI

- Talks held between Viet Minh leaders and Laotian and Cambodian rebel chiefs.

- Democratic Republic of Vietnam recognized by Mao Tse-tung.

- Ho Chi Minh's rebel Communist regime recognized by the Soviet Union as Vietnam's legal government.

- Parisians demonstrate against Soviet recognition of Ho Chi Minh's government.

- French forces in North Vietnam come under severe fire from the Communists - appeal to the U.S. for military support.

- France is given U.S. military aid to guard against Ho Chi Minh and Mao Tse-tung alliance.

- Independence is granted within the French Union to Vietnam, Laos and Cambodia by France despite loud Communist opposition. Bao Dai heads the independent government of Vietnam headquartered in Saigon.

WHAT A YEAR IT WAS!

1950

BRITAIN

CHURCHILL WARNS OF WORLD WAR III THREAT.

DESPITE U.S. PROTESTS, GREAT BRITAIN INITIATES RESTRICTIONS ON IMPORTS OF AMERICAN FUEL OIL AND GASOLINE.

KING GEORGE VI AGREES TO DISSOLVE PARLIAMENT AND TO HOLD GENERAL ELECTIONS.

LABOR PARTY WINS GENERAL ELECTIONS.

PRIME MINISTER CLEMENT R. ATTLEE HEADS NEW BRITISH CABINET.

UNITED NATIONS

Soviet motion to oust Nationalist China defeated by U.N.

Soviet Union.

Soviet proposal for vote on German reunification turned down by the West.

U.N. General Assembly defeats Soviet-Indian proposal to allow Communist China into any U.N. division.

Jacob Malik of the Soviet Union leaves a U.N. Security Council meeting in protest of Chinese representative T.F. Tsiang.

The U.S. and France outraged over England's recognition of the Communist People's Republic of China.

⊛ First shipments of one billion dollars in aid for Europe leaves from Norfolk, Virginia.

⊛ Belgium's King Leopold is returned to power in a referendum vote after a 6-year exile. Mounting protests force him to abdicate the throne in favor of his son Baudouin.

⊛ French government announces dismissal of Communist Dr. Frederic Joliot Curie as chief of the Atomic Energy Commission.

⊛ U.S. resumes relations with Spain.

500,000 Germans Gather In West Berlin On May Day To Condemn Communism.

Bonn Is Granted Right To Set Its Own Foreign Policy By Allies.

President Truman names Lt. General Walter B. Smith director of the C.I.A.

Anna M. Rosenberg of New York is appointed Assistant Defense Secretary in charge of manpower and personnel policy.

New York's Mayor William O'Dwyer appointed U.S. Ambassador to Mexico by President Truman effective after his resignation as mayor.

Passings

Politician, author and forward-thinker **Leon Blum**, the first Jewish and Socialist Prime Minister of France, who was sent to a German concentration camp during World War II and returned to politics after the war, dies at age 77.

Former three-term Massachusetts

Fitzgerald

congressman and two-term mayor of Boston, **John Francis "Honey Fitz" Fitzgerald**, father of Rose Kennedy, dies at the age of 87.

America's first woman senator, **Hattie Wyatt Caraway** dies at age 72.

ELSIE'S SPRING TRIO — 3 dishes—2 "hots" and a "sweet"

Rice'n everything nice
including eggs, mushrooms and creamy
Borden's Evaporated Milk

4 tablespoons butter or margarine
¼ cup flour   ½ teaspoon salt
¼ teaspoon dry mustard
1 teaspoon Worcestershire sauce
1 14½-oz. can Borden's
Evaporated Milk   1 cup water
1 cup cooked mushrooms, sliced
5 hard cooked eggs, quartered
1 cup Borden's grated American Cheese

Melt butter or margarine, add flour, salt, mustard, Worcestershire sauce, blending until smooth. Stir in Borden's concentrated, double-rich Evaporated Milk (notice how smooth and easily Borden's Evaporated Milk blends) and water; cook over boiling water, stirring until thickened. Add cheese, stir until melted. Add mushrooms and eggs. Turn into center of rice ring or serve on toast. Makes 6 servings.

Old fashioned good coffee without cooking
Borden's Instant Coffee

Here's the coffee that has rich flavor . . . magic convenience . . . and real economy, too. Yes, Borden's saves you up to 20¢ against a pound of ground coffee.

You'll love Borden's. It is 100% pure percolated coffee . . . concentrated in powder form; all the grounds are thrown away. No bulky fillers are added . . . no carbohydrates or dextrose to dilute the precious flavor.

So don't be fooled by the size of the jar! You get as many cups from the regular size jar of Borden's as you do from a pound of ground coffee! The large 5 oz. jar gives you as many cups as 2½ pounds of ground, and saves you up to 50¢. Order Borden's Instant Coffee today. For real coffee pleasure every time, serve Borden's every meal.

Scrumptious Boston Dream Pie
Another "Magic Recipe" by
Borden's Eagle Brand

Make cake from prepared mix and turn into a greased 8-inch square pan. Bake as directed. With knife cut almost to bottom of cake 1 inch from edge. Lift out center and fill hollow. *Filling:*

1⅓ cups (15 oz. can) Eagle
Brand Sweetened
Condensed Milk
½ cup lemon juice
1 teaspoon grated lemon rind
2 egg yolks
confectioners' sugar

Combine all ingredients except sugar and blend. Fill hollow and replace top. Sprinkle top with confectioners' sugar using paper doily to make design. Serves 8.

FREE! "Eagle Brand MAGIC Recipes"—Address Elsie, Dept. S-30, Box 175, New York 46, N. Y.

© THE BORDEN COMPANY

IF IT'S BORDEN'S—IT'S GOT TO BE GOOD!

PEOPLE

On The Carpet With Queen Mary

Queen Mary's amazing energy at the age of 82 is well known but her latest accomplishment has astonished the world.

This magnificent hand-embroidered carpet made by the Queen herself was begun in 1941 and contains at least a million stitches representing 3,000 hours of skilled work.

The intricate pattern of each of the 12 panels speaks for itself. Fine wools of a hundred different shades were used to produce this outstanding work of art.

Each panel bears the signature of Her Majesty.

27

1950

Wallis Simpson

The Metropolitan Museum Of Art's Costume Institute Receives "Wallis Blue" — The Duchess Of Windsor's 1937 Wedding Dress.

GUNS & ICING ON THE CAKE

Queen Elizabeth Celebrates Her 50th Birthday With Artillery Salutes Throughout The Kingdom And Cake With Pink And White Icing.

OH, FRANKIE

Frank Sinatra Croons "If I Loved You" At The Request Of Princess Margaret During A Kensington Garden Party In London. He Is Impressed With The Princess' Musical Knowledge And How Hep She Is.

THE ROYALS GO TO THE THEATRE

For the first time in its 132-year history, the **Old Vic** has royalty in the house as **Queen Elizabeth, Princess Margaret** and **King George VI** attend a performance of **Twelfth Night**.

Japan's **Crown Prince Akihito** starts his junior year in high school.

THE ROYALS VISIT THE ROYALS

England's King George And Queen Elizabeth Make Elaborate Arrangements To Welcome The Netherlands' Queen Juliana And Her Husband Prince Bernhard On Their State Visit To Britain.

Marrying An American Medical Student Costs **Iran's Princess Fatima** All Her Royal Privileges.

Sweden's **Gustav VI** Takes The Throne When His Dad King Gustav V Dies At 92.

23-Year Old Grandson Of King **Chulalongkorn** Is Crowned Rama IX In Thailand.

I Say, I Said LOOK AT THE BIRDIE, Not GRAB THE BIRDIE

Royal photographer **Cecil Beaton** shoots first pictures of **Princess Elizabeth's** second child, **Princess Anne**, despite first born, 22-month old **Prince Charles'** attempts to remove the "birdie" from the camera.

WHAT A YEAR IT WAS!

What a Merry Christmas gift!
The beautiful GENERAL ELECTRIC
COMBINATION SANDWICH GRILL AND WAFFLE IRON!

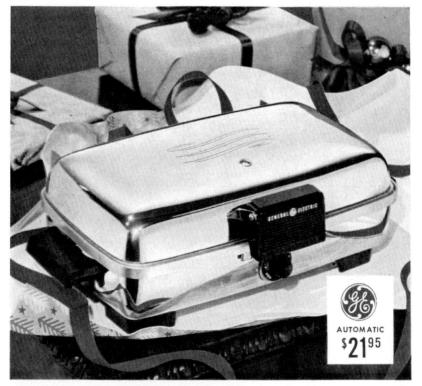

See your G-E dealer. $21.95. *Prices subject to change without notice.*

AUTOMATIC
$21.95

IT'LL BE a Merry Christmas indeed—if someone's thoughtful enough to give you the so-beautiful, so-convenient General Electric Combination Sandwich Grill and Waffle Iron!

You toast delicious sandwiches . . . make tempting, golden waffles (simply by inserting the large interchangeable aluminum waffle grids) . . . even fry bacon and eggs—*all right at your table!*

That's right! With the wonderful new General Electric Combination Sandwich Grill and Waffle Iron, there's no fussing at the range, no dashing to and from the kitchen to serve dishes nice and hot!

Finished in sparkling, long-lasting chrome plate, equipped with cool plastic handles, the new Combination Sandwich Grill and Waffle Iron is so beautiful it will adorn your loveliest table setting. And its graceful, streamlined design makes it so easy to clean, too!

Automatic, a turn of the Temperature Selector quickly gives you the right heat. A "tell-you-when" light goes off the second you have it. And for added convenience, when the appliance is not in use, you wrap the cord around the grill and secure it with the new G-E cord latch.

Automatic model (illustrated)—and the Standard model at $16.95—come complete with both sandwich *and* waffle grids. Also a booklet with a new, taste-delighting recipe for every day in the month. You'll want to use them *all* on Christmas day! General Electric Company, Bridgeport 2, Connecticut.

For a wonderful *luncheon treat*, toast delicious sandwiches—*right at your table!*

Larger grids make four *waffles* at a time to reduce waiting to a minimum!

You can put your confidence in—

GENERAL ⊕ ELECTRIC

29

The Nation Bids Farewell
General Who Dies Of

One of the nation's first three military aviators, **GENERAL HENRY "Hap" ARNOLD** returns to the capital of a nation which he served long and brilliantly.

After 40 years of service he retired to the quiet life on his ranch in California.

General Arnold rose to head the world's mightiest military armada. Under his guidance Germany and Japan were crushed and he paved the way for ultimate victory.

WHAT A YEAR IT WAS!

To Its First Five-Star Air
A Heart Attack At 63

Military comrades including Chief of Staff **George Marshall** *(left)* and **General Eisenhower** pay tribute to the man who with them was an architect of victory.

GENERAL ARNOLD receives all the military honors of the nation's military greats.

People line the streets to pay their respects.

For all those who shared the burden of America's defense, his passing means the loss of a friend and to America it means the loss of one of her finest soldiers.

Hedy Lamarr

GOOD NEWS FOR FENCERS

HOLLYWOOD SCREEN STAR HEDY LAMARR reports that $250,000 in jewelry has been stolen from her suite at the Sherry Netherlands Hotel.

$6,000 IN JEWELS IS STOLEN FROM LUCILLE BALL AND DESI ARNAZ'S hotel room in Chicago including a 40-carat aquamarine ring.

BILLY ROSE AND HIS WIFE ELEANOR HOLM discover $25,000 in jewelry missing from their Manhattan town home on returning from the theatre. Fortunately, Eleanor was wearing $250,000 in baubles to the opening.

A Miffed **KATHERINE HEPBURN** Is Arrested Along With Her Chauffeur Near **Blackwell, Oklahoma** For **Driving 80 Miles An Hour**.

ROBIN AND HIS FOUR HOODS

Underworld star **Mickey Cohen** and some of his associates are found innocent on conspiracy charges stemming from an alleged plot to assault radio repairman Alfred Pearson (who tried to foreclose on a widow's home). Cohen receives a standing ovation from courtroom spectators.

HEY, NOW YOU'RE MESSIN' WITH MY SOOTS!

Mobster **Mickey Cohen** has his sleep interrupted once again when some of his gangster enemies dynamite his $100,000 Brentwood, California home for the second time this year destroying his wardrobe.

Mickey Cohen

BUBBLE, BUBBLE, TOIL & TROUBLE

Fan Dancer **Sally Rand** Refuses To State Her Age After Being Arrested For Indecent Exposure In Milwaukee.

PUTTING HIS ICE ON THE ICE BLOCK

With two of his aides — **Frank Niccoli** and **Dave Ogul** — jumping bail, mobster **Mickey Cohen** puts $150,000 in jewelry and silverware on the auction block to raise $25,000 needed to make good on the bond.

I REFUSE TO ANSWER ON THE GROUNDS THAT I MIGHT WIND UP IN A CEMENT MIXER

Underworld's **Meyer Lansky** refuses to answer questions before Senator Estes Kefauver's crime investigating committee regarding a $26,000,000 interstate gambling operation.

WHAT A YEAR IT WAS!

"I SPY"

Mildred E. Gillars, alias **Axis Sally**, in prison for aiding and abetting the enemy (Nazi Germany) during World War II, loses her appeal in U.S. Court of Appeals and will continue serving her 10-30 year sentence.

Klaus Fuchs is sentenced to 14 years in London for spying and passing atom bomb secrets to the Soviets.

A-Bomb spy **Harry Gold** receives 30-year sentence for his World War II secret agent activities with convicted spy Klaus Fuchs.

Asking for leniency in a Hungarian court, American **Robert Vogeler** confesses that he is a spy. He is sentenced to 15 years in prison.

Rosenberg

Julius Rosenberg is arrested by the FBI in New York on charges of conspiracy to commit espionage for the U.S.S.R. **Miriam Moskowitz** and **Abraham Brothman** are arrested later in Cliftwood, New Jersey on the same charges as is **Morton Sobell** in Laredo, Texas.

Failing to reveal his Communist ties at his naturalization hearing in San Francisco lands **Harry Bridges** five years in jail.

"**T**he Aldrich Family" cast member **Jean Muir** is dropped from the show after being accused of Communist affiliation.

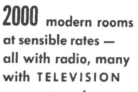
NOBEL PEACE PRIZE

RALPH J. BUNCHE
USA

Famous Birth

Princess Anne

PASSINGS

Robert Ringling, second generation member of the famed circus family and former opera singer who eventually became chairman of the board of Ringling Brothers and Barnum & Bailey Combined Shows, Inc., dies at age 52.

Explorer, author, publisher and widower of Amelia Earhart, **George Palmer Putnam** dies at 62 in Trona, California.

Frances Seymour Brokaw Fonda, estranged wife of Henry, mother of Jane and Peter, takes her own life in Beacon, New York at age 42.

Indian mystic, guru and philosopher **Sri Aurobindo** dies at age 78.

Coupling

CAN THIS YOUNG GIRL FROM A SMALL MINING TOWN IN NOBLESTOWN, PA. STAY MARRIED TO THE MOST ELIGIBLE BACHELOR OF 1948?

After Less Than Two Years Of Marriage, The Former Coal Miner's Daughter Barbara "Bobo" Rockefeller *And Her Multi-Millionaire Husband* Winthrop *Separate Because Of Many Disagreements.*

❦

FIRST YOU SAY YOU DO THEN YOU SAY YOU DON'T

18-Year Old Beautiful Actress Elizabeth Taylor *Weds Hotel Heir* Conrad Hilton, Jr. *In Beverly Hills As 700 Of Hollywood's Most Famous Witness The Services In The Church Of The Good Shepherd.*

❦

After What Is One Of The Hollywood Weddings Of The Year, Liz And Nicky *Announce Their Separation.*

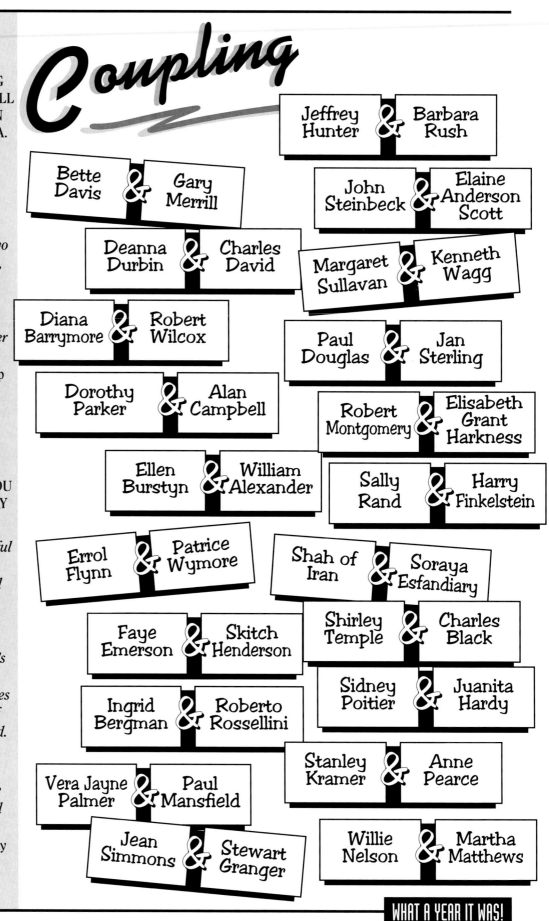

Jeffrey Hunter & Barbara Rush

Bette Davis & Gary Merrill

John Steinbeck & Elaine Anderson Scott

Deanna Durbin & Charles David

Margaret Sullavan & Kenneth Wagg

Diana Barrymore & Robert Wilcox

Paul Douglas & Jan Sterling

Dorothy Parker & Alan Campbell

Robert Montgomery & Elisabeth Grant Harkness

Ellen Burstyn & William Alexander

Sally Rand & Harry Finkelstein

Errol Flynn & Patrice Wymore

Shah of Iran & Soraya Esfandiary

Faye Emerson & Skitch Henderson

Shirley Temple & Charles Black

Ingrid Bergman & Roberto Rossellini

Sidney Poitier & Juanita Hardy

Stanley Kramer & Anne Pearce

Vera Jayne Palmer & Paul Mansfield

Jean Simmons & Stewart Granger

Willie Nelson & Martha Matthews

WHAT A YEAR IT WAS!

UNCOUPLING

Sir Anthony Eden & Beatrice Helen Eden

Bette Davis & William Grant Sherry

Jackie Coogan & Ann McCormack Coogan

Betty Hutton & Ted Briskin

Elliott Roosevelt & Faye Emerson

Joan Blondell & Michael Todd

Gloria De Haven & John Payne

John Huston & Evelyn Keyes

Groucho Marx & Kay Dittig Gorcey

Milton Berle & Joyce Matthews

Hattie McDaniel & Larry Williams

Myrna Loy & Gene Markey

Ingmar Bergman & Ellen Lundstrom

Robert Montgomery & Betty Montgomery

Ingrid Bergman & Dr. Peter Lindstrom

Roberto Rossellini & Marcella de Marchis

Frank Sinatra & Ava Gardner

WANDERING OL' BLUE EYES

Nancy Sinatra Is Awarded A Legal Separation From Frank On The Grounds Of Mental Cruelty Stating That He Leaves Her On The Weekends. Can Ava Gardner Be Far Away?

♥

THE SWASHBUCKLER & THE TEENAGER & THE GIRLFRIEND & THE EX-WIFE — A TRUE HOLLYWOOD TALE

41-Year Old Screen Actor Errol Flynn *Still Plans To Marry 19-Year Old Rumanian Princess* Irene Ghica *In Paris. In The Meantime, Kansas Oilman* James Wymore *Announces His Daughter, Actress* Patrice, *23, Is Engaged To* Flynn *While* Flynn's *Ex-Wife Hauls His Two-Timing Swashbuckling Hide Into Court Over An Alimony Dispute.*

JUST THE HOUSEWORK MA'AM

Jack Webb's beautiful wife **Julie London** turns down movie contract on the grounds that her career is less important than her role as a wife, mother and homemaker and that she would in no way compete with the star of *Dragnet*.

A WIMP IN PADDED CLOTHING

Ginger Rogers says that those men who criticize women for wearing falsies should take a good look at their own shoulder pads. What a woman sees isn't necessarily what she's going to get when that jacket comes off, as sometimes what looks like a hunk turns out to be a little wimp in padded clothing.

TEA BAGS & TAIL SPINS

By presidential appointment, radio personality **Arthur Godfrey** is now full Commander in the Naval Air Reserve.

War hero **Audie Murphy** says *The Red Badge Of Courage* is his last picture as he's giving up his movie career.

Air Secretary W. Stuart Symington presents **Bob Hope** with the Air Force's Exceptional Service Award for his unending efforts in entertaining our servicemen stationed overseas.

Bob Hope and **Jane Russell** make opening day box-office history at the Paramount—selling more tickets than any other opening day in the theatre's 23-year history.

IN SEARCH OF THE NEXT RAINBOW

MGM releases JUDY GARLAND from her contract after 15 years of making films together.

Beautiful Screen Star GREER GARSON Applies For U.S. Citizenship In Fort Worth, Texas.

British Actor CHARLES LAUGHTON And His Wife ELSA LANCHESTER Become American Citizens.

TOO **FAT** TO BE THE **FAT MAN**?

Radio's star of **The Fat Man**, **Jack Smart**, eats a few too many cheese blintzes and can't get through the door of his Hollywood dressing room, sit in a make-up chair or—horrors of all horrors—fit in the camera range for a close-up.

Duke Ellington loses 16 pounds during his 11-week European concert tour by giving up "coffee, tea and water in Germany," and sticking to that famous German beer.

LET'S SEE THOSE GAMS BABY

Joan Crawford poses for another cheesecake shot bringing the total number of times she displays her legs for photographers to around 800.

MILDRED TURNER — FAMOUS SWEATER GIRL (What's Wrong With This Name?)

Idahoan Julia Jean Mildred Frances Turner officially changes her name to LANA TURNER in Hollywood.

YOU WANT TO PUT MY *WHAT* IN THE CEMENT??

Despite urging from her fans that she imprint other parts of her famous anatomy, Hollywood's *Sweater Girl*, LANA TURNER, only imprints her hand and footprints in front of Grauman's Chinese Theatre.

Lana Turner

WHAT A YEAR IT WAS!

YOU BETTER WASH MY NAME RIGHT OUT OF YOUR HEAD

Procter & Gamble settles **Tallulah Bankhead's** $1,000,000 lawsuit over using her name for a shampoo in a radio jingle for $5,000.

Dean Martin & Jerry Lewis file suit against their agent's wife for mismanagement of their money.

Screen tough guy **Edward G. Robinson** makes an appearance before the House Committee On Un-American Activities to deny any Communist connections.

REDHEADS GET THE BEAUTY NOD FROM THOSE WHO BOB

According to a famous Hollywood beauty salon, redheads are the world's sexiest women including beautiful natural redheads **Susan Hayward, Rhonda Fleming** *and* **Ann Sheridan.** *Other gorgeous dye-job redheads include* **Rita Hayworth, Ava Gardner, Janet Blair** *and* **Ellen Drew.**

Wearing the traditional cap and gown, **Elizabeth Taylor** *receives her high school diploma.*

AND ON A DIFFERENT NOTE

68-year old conductor **Leopold Stokowski** *and his wife* **Gloria Vanderbilt** *produce their first child.*

A fan of **Lauren Bacall's** *is arrested and released for the second time in a year when he is found on the grounds of her Benedict Canyon home.*

Despite critical acclaim for his acting in A Streetcar Named Desire *and* The Men, **Marlon Brando** *is uncertain about continuing his acting career because of what he perceives as the untruths in acting.*

38-year old **Lucille Ball** *& 33-year old* **Desi Arnaz** *celebrate their 10th wedding anniversary backstage at New York's Roxy Theatre where they are appearing.*

Robert Frost Celebrates His 75th Birthday.

Greatest Living Jazzman, **Louis "Satchmo" Armstrong** Celebrates His 50th Birthday In New York.

COME UP AND EAT IN MY PLACE SOMETIME

Mae West's Diamond Lil Casino And Restaurant Scheduled To Be Built In *Las Vegas* At An Estimated Cost Of $1,000,000.

NOW DON'T DUMMY UP ON ME

Edgar Bergen And **Charlie McCarthy** Star At The New Desert Inn Hotel In *Las Vegas.*

Edgar & Charlie

YOU DON'T HAVE TO BE JEWISH TO BE A PRINCESS

RITA HAYWORTH and **PRINCE ALY KHAN** have a new 5-lb. baby daughter—Princess Yasmin—born in Lausanne, Switzerland.

HOLIDAY VALUE SALE!

Floral Plastic Tablecloth

WHITE LACE DESIGN—FULL SIZE

$1.50 Value
Yours for Only 50¢

WITH TWO WRAPPERS OR BOX TOPS FROM ANY OF THESE LEVER PRODUCTS

Ask Your Grocer about this Sensational Value!
Finest Quality—Resists Stains—Wipes Clean Instantly with a Damp Cloth—Never Needs Washing or Ironing!

Now...glamorize your daytime meals and dinette dinners with this smart, practical table cover of clear, sparkling plastic cloth. It's a gorgeous floral pattern.

It's hard to believe this handsome table cover is actually yours for only 50¢ and 2 box tops or wrappers from any of the fine Lever products illustrated. This handsome cloth is a certified $1.50 value. It's full-size approximately 54 x 54 inches—just right for dinette, breakfast or card table.

Use it right over your table top or as a cover to protect your finest linen cloths. Saves laundry. Wonderful for families with small children. Wipes

clean with a damp cloth. Never needs washing or ironing. Fully stain-resistant!

An Amazing Value—Will Be Offered Only Once

Go to your grocer's now and stock up on LUX FLAKES, LUX TOILET SOAP, LIFEBUOY, RINSO and SILVER DUST. Send 2 box tops or wrappers from any of these fine Lever products with 50¢ for each tablecloth you order. Get several.

They make marvelous gifts—and are grand for your own entertaining during the holidays and the year 'round. But hurry. Get yours while the supply lasts. Use the handy order blank on this page. Get additional blanks from your grocer — and send them in without delay.

Use This Handy Order Form TODAY

Mail to TABLECLOTH, Box No. 730, New York 46, N.Y.

I enclose _____ in cash and _____ wrappers or box tops from any of these Lever Products:

**RINSO   SILVER DUST   LUX FLAKES
LUX TOILET SOAP   LIFEBUOY**

Please send ____ FLORAL PLASTIC TABLECLOTHS
To:

Name_____

Address_____

City_____ Zone_____ State_____

This offer is good only in the continental United States (including Alaska), and Hawaii. Expires January 31, 1951. Allow 3 weeks for delivery. This offer is subject to applicable state and local regulations.

38

Starring In MEDICAL ROLES

EVITA PERON, Wife Of Argentine President Juan, Has Her Appendix Removed.

Marilyn Monroe Attempts Suicide With Overdose Of Barbiturates.

Judy Garland Is Feeling Better And Has Gone Fishing In Sun Valley, Idaho With Her Daughter Lisa After Recovering From Throat Wounds Self Inflicted With A Piece Of Broken Glass.

Following Her Return To The U.S. After A European Tour, **DOROTHY LAMOUR** Is Hospitalized In Los Angeles For Fatigue And Removal Of An Abdominal Cyst.

Just As Her Cracked Vertebra Is Healing **CLAUDETTE COLBERT** Slips Again, This Time Rupturing A Disc.

Rita Hayworth Faints In Paris Knocking A Bottle Of Wine Over Onto **Maurice Chevalier's** New Tuxedo. He Yells That His New Suit Is Ruined, And After She Is Revived, Miss Hayworth Offers To Pay For The Dry Cleaning.

THE SHOW ALWAYS GOES ON

Despite A Fractured Wrist Suffered In A Fall In Portland, Maine, **LYNN FONTANNE** Performs With Her Husband **ALFRED LUNT** In *I Know My Love*.

IN FOR ANOTHER TAPING

Poor **PAUL DOUGLAS**. After Suffering A Rib Injury While Shooting A Football Scene, He's Back At The Doctor's For Yet Another Taping Of His Ribs After Completing A Rather Energetic Love Scene With **LINDA DARNELL**.

THE BROTHERS EISENHOWER

Their Momma Would Really Be Proud As **DWIGHT D. EISENHOWER** (President Of Columbia University) And **MILTON EISENHOWER** (President Of Penn State College) Both Receive Honorary Doctor Of Laws Degrees From Temple University.

Columbia University President General **DWIGHT D. EISENHOWER** Named Commander-In-Chief Of NATO Forces By **PRESIDENT TRUMAN.**

Eisenhower

GENERAL EISENHOWER Decides To Return To His Farming Roots And Buys A 179-Acre Spread For $23,000 Near The Gettysburg, Pa. Civil War Battleground.

THIS AIN'T NO BULL

Winston Churchill's favorite cow, Gratwicke Beatrice II, wins first prize at the Kent agricultural show.

First lady of the world, **Eleanor Roosevelt**, receives the Four Freedoms Award for her distinguished service.

Eleanor Roosevelt is nominated by President Truman for a new three-year term as U.S. representative on the U.N. Human Rights Commission of the Economic and Social Council.

A WOMAN'S PLACE IS STILL IN THE HOUSE — AND WE DON'T MEAN THE WHITE HOUSE

Eleanor Roosevelt says the nation is not yet ready to elect a woman president.

WHAT DO YOU MEAN SHE HIT A CLINKER?

Angered over a critic's pan of his daughter Margaret's singing, **President Truman** threatens to slug it out with him.

President of the National Cartoonists Society, Milton Caniff (*Steve Canyon*) bestows honorary membership in the society on **President Truman** despite the president's confession that he can't draw.

General Douglas MacArthur receives the Distinguished Service Medal from President Truman.

THE ANSWER MY DEAR IS IN THE STARS

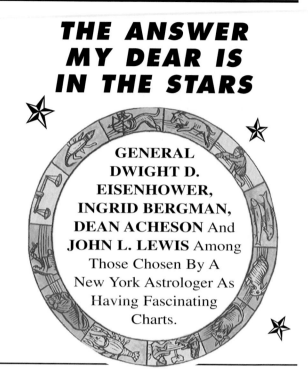

GENERAL DWIGHT D. EISENHOWER, INGRID BERGMAN, DEAN ACHESON And **JOHN L. LEWIS** Among Those Chosen By A New York Astrologer As Having Fascinating Charts.

SINGING FOR "C" NOTES

Ex-Red spy **Whittaker Chambers** to be paid $75,000 by *The Saturday Evening Post* for revealing the whole story.

An appellate division ruling disbars **Alger Hiss** from practicing law in New York.

Nelson A. Rockefeller, 42, is named chairman of the advisory board of the Point Four project.

A HAIRY SUBJECT

Bald Colorado Republican **Senator Eugene D. Millikin** objects to senators such as **Robert A. Taft** covering up their bald spots on the grounds it's deceitful which he feels has no place in politics.

Ireland's premier comes to New York to gain support against Ireland being partitioned.

Hotel magnate **Conrad Hilton** receives the Brotherhood Award of the National Conference of Christians and Jews for distinguished civic service.

U.S. Minister to Luxembourg, **Perle Mesta** is named "Woman of the Year" by an Associated Press poll of women editors of American newspapers.

Miss
Europe

**Hanní
Schall**

IT'S NOT ALL GREEK TO HIM

Israel's Prime Minister **DAVID BEN-GURION**, A Greek Scholar, Takes His First Trip Abroad Since Israel Became A State And Is Off To Greece To Inspect Several Archaeological Digs.

 60% OF THE WOMEN Listed In **Who's Who In America** Are Married Or Have Been Married.

EDITH S. SAMPSON Becomes First Negro* Appointed To A U.S. Assembly Delegation To The United Nations.

TURNING 80 IN A FEW HOURS, BERNARD M. BARUCH Is Sworn In As Honorary Commissioner Of Borough Works In Manhattan.

DR. ALBERT EINSTEIN Donates The Original Manuscript Of His New **"Generalized Theory Of Gravitation"** To The Hebrew University In Jerusalem.

* Negro was the commonly-used term in 1950.

PORTRAIT OF A FALLEN PEACE EFFORT

PABLO PICASSO *Is Among A 12-Man Peace Delegation* Denied Entry Visas By The U.S. State Department Because Of Their Communist Affiliations.

SALT & KETCHUP ON YOUR EGGS MONSIEUR?

(THROW IT AGAINST THE WALL AND SEE IF IT STICKS)

On returning to Paris after a visit to America, Surrealist artist **SALVADOR DALI** notes that the light for painting is poor and the food barbaric.

Dali

Former Boxing Champ
Jack Dempsey
Passes His
California Real Estate Brokers' Exam.

DOING FANCY FOOTWORK WITHOUT THE PUNCH
Rocky Graziano
Former Middleweight Champ
Is Dancing To A Different Tune
As He Changes Careers And Becomes A
Dance Teacher In The **Wally Wanger Dancing School** In New York.

1950

America's 10 Most Beautiful Women

LINDA DARNELL
OLIVIA DE HAVILLAND
AVA GARDNER
GREER GARSON
MARY PICKFORD
GINGER ROGERS
ELIZABETH TAYLOR
LORETTA YOUNG
MRS. ALFRED G. VANDERBILT
ESTHER WILLIAMS

More Famous Beauties...
MRS. HARRISON WILLIAMS
COLLEEN TOWNSEND
MARGARET PHELAN
MRS. WILLIAM O'DWYER

The Most Beautiful Shoulders In Hollywood
MAUREEN O'HARA
LINDA DARNELL

THE MOST ADMIRED AND INFLUENTIAL WOMEN

Sister Elizabeth **Kenny**
Claire Booth **Luce**
Emily **Post**
Eleanor **Roosevelt**
Dorothy **Thompson**
Helen **Keller**
Margaret **Truman**
Madame Chiang **Kai-shek**

THE GREATEST MEN IN WORLD HISTORY (A German POLL)

WINSTON CHURCHILL

CHANCELLOR BISMARCK

ADOLPH HITLER

A UNANIMOUS DECISION

Supreme Court Justice **William O. Douglas** Is Named **Father Of The Year**.

American **Mother Of The Year** Is **Mrs. Henry Roe Cloud**, Part Indian And Mother Of Four Daughters.

TEN GREATEST JEWS OF THE FIRST HALF of THE CENTURY

Albert Einstein	(Theoretical Physicist)
David Ben-Gurion	(Israeli Prime Minister)
Sigmund Freud	(Physician and Pioneer Psychoanalyst)
Louis D. Brandeis	(U.S. Supreme Court Justice)
Leon Trotsky	(Russian Revolutionary, Soviet Statesman)
Stephen S. Wise	(Rabbi)
Chaim Weizmann	(Chemist and Statesman)
Israel Zangwill	(British Novelist)
Leon Blum	(French Author and Socialist Leader)
Chaim Nachman Bialik	(Hebrew Poet)

CATCH A FALLING STAR

Claudette Colbert Is Selected Most Favorite Star By The WOMAN'S HOME COMPANION Pushing Last Year's First Place Favorite Ingrid Bergman To #10.

PEOPLE MOST ADMIRED BY TEEN-AGERS

Joe DiMaggio

Abraham Lincoln

Louisa May Alcott

Franklin D. Roosevelt

Roy Rogers

Vera-Ellen

Babe Ruth

Douglas MacArthur

Clara Barton

Doris Day

Florence Nightingale

KEEPING FIT
A CROSS-SECTION OF AMERICAN MEN

Dean Acheson (Secretary of State)	*Does outdoor work on his farm.*
J. Edgar Hoover (Head of FBI)	*Long walks, garden work, proper diet.*
Robert R. Young (Chairman of the Board, Chesapeake & Ohio)	*Exercise, balanced diet, nap after lunch.*
Charles E. Wilson (President, General Electric)	*Mixture of hard work, exercise and interest in other people.*
Fred Allen (Humorist)	*Handball.*
James A. Michener (Novelist)	*Volleyball, tennis.*
Ezio Pinza (Star of "South Pacific")	*Good diet, long daily walks.*
Gary Cooper (Actor)	*Daily tennis, skiing, proper diet & sleep.*

MOST ELIGIBLE BACHELORS IN AMERICA
According To BARBIZON MODELS

Marlon **BRANDO**

Montgomery **CLIFT**

Joe **DIMAGGIO**

Paul **DOUGLAS**

Howard **DUFF**

Farley **GRANGER**

Peter **LAWFORD**

Edgar **LUCKENBACH**

Robert **MERRILL**

H. L. MENCKEN is named **FIRST HONORARY MEMBER** *Of The* **Beer-Of-The-Month Club**

TIME THE AMERICAN FIGHTING MAN — MAN OF THE YEAR

☆ **Margaret Truman** considered *Nation's #1 Bachelor Girl.*

☆ The Malibu Lions Club names actress **June Havoc** *"All-Year Queen Of Malibu."*

☆ Primitive painter **Grandma Moses** voted *Grandmother-Of-The-Year* by the Cambridge, New York Lions Club.

☆ **Loretta Young** and **Alan Ladd** voted *Most Cooperative Stars* by the Hollywood Women's Press Club while **Olivia de Havilland** and **Robert Mitchum** receive *Least Cooperative* honors.

☆ **Ernest Hemingway** (masculinity), **Ava Gardner** (passion) and **Yogi Berra** (primal—most down-to-earth face) chosen as some of *America's Most Stimulating Faces* by the National Association of Women Artists.

☆ Former Republican representative from Connecticut, **Clare Boothe Luce** names **Eleanor Roosevelt** the *Best-Loved Woman in the World* at a dinner given in the former First Lady's honor.

☆ Bandleader **Guy Lombardo** is dubbed *"Mr. Peter Cottontail of 1950"* by the American Rabbit and Coney Dealers Association.

FOXES in general have less massive teeth than other members of the canine family. Shown here is a Red Fox, distinguished by its rusty red fur, black-fronted forelegs and white-tipped tail.

The Prairie Wolf, or COYOTE, differs from other wolves in its smaller size and fox-like head.

THE "TRADE-MARKS" OF NATURE*

mark the difference in canines...

*Prepared in cooperation with specialists of American Museum of Natural History, N.Y.

THE TRADE-MARK "ETHYL"

marks the important difference in gasoline

The WOLF is the largest wild member of the canine family. It also has the largest teeth. Shown here is a Gray Wolf.

The GERMAN SHEPHERD, or German Police dog, resembles a wolf—but the dog has shorter hair, less mane and a smaller head in proportion to the body.

The JACKAL is distinguished by a fox-like appearance and by being more richly colored than the wolf. For example, the African Black-Backed Jackal shown here has a black back, reddish sides and white underparts.

ENJOY THE DIFFERENCE!

Just fill your tank with gasoline from an "Ethyl" pump and feel the difference for yourself. Because "Ethyl" gasoline averages *five full octane numbers higher* than regular gasoline, it will bring out the full power and performance of your car. And because it has, on the average, a higher volatility, it will give you faster starting and warm-up.

When you see the familiar yellow-and-black "Ethyl" emblem on a pump, you know you are getting the best gasoline your service station offers—gasoline that is improved with "Ethyl" antiknock fluid, the famous ingredient that steps up power and performance.

"Ethyl" products are made by ETHYL CORPORATION, Chrysler Bldg., New York 17, N. Y.

Human Interest

The 1950 Cancer Crusade

Bing Crosby makes an appeal to moviegoers to support this year's Cancer Drive.

"We must open our minds to the truth that may save our lives and our hearts to the Cancer Crusade appeal…Let's strike back at cancer. Your part in this campaign is to place your contribution in an envelope and mail to 'Cancer,'… Do it today."

New York Fashion Show Benefit For The March Of Dimes

Hundreds of people pay $25 to $50 a seat to attend this worthy cause to raise funds for victims of infantile paralysis.

Lillian Gish and Mrs. Randolph Hearst *(top, left)* are in attendance along with foundation president Basil O'Connor and Helen Hayes *(top, right)* and such social leaders as Bobo Rockefeller *(left)*.

*A*nyone who is anyone shows up for this glittering event and the fashions span the old to the new.

Poster girl Wanda Wiley is a reminder that last year infantile paralysis hit a record high.

"South Pacific" star Ezio Pinza joins in the effort to make this year the Year Of Hope in The March of Dimes war against polio.

WHAT A YEAR IT WAS!

Are you now or have you ever been...

Overriding President Truman's veto, Congress passes the Mundt Bill designed to compel Communist organizations to identify their officers and account for how they spend their money.

Eleven Communist leaders lose appeal in U.S. Court of Appeals on their conviction of conspiring to teach and advocate the overthrow of the U.S. Government.

Congress receives Master Civil Defense Plan from President Truman.

Under the Internal Security Act, the Justice Department begins national roundup of 86 leading U.S. alien Communists for deportation.

In a Supreme Court ruling questions about Communist ties do not have to be answered on grounds of self-incrimination.

Visitors from totalitarian nations banned visas by U.S. State Department.

Dwight D. Eisenhower's book Crusade In Europe is banned in the Soviet zone of Austria on the grounds that it is fascist literature.

The Franklin D. Roosevelt Library makes papers available for research purposes.

The 22nd AMENDMENT To The U.S. Constitution Is Passed Limiting Presidents To Two Terms.

The presidential election system is changed by the U.S. Senate dividing each state's Electoral Votes among candidates in proportion to popular vote.

Famous Births
Cathy Guisewaite
Gary Larson

Republican Senator William Langer of North Dakota introduces bill outlawing interstate transmission of alcoholic beverage advertising.

During an arrest, police are now permitted to search a limited area for evidence without a search warrant according to a U.S. Supreme Court ruling.

The House of Representatives approves U.S. admission of Alaska and Hawaii.

BALLOTS & BAGELS

Colorado passes bill allowing Jewish people to vote by absentee ballot in its primary election which falls on the Jewish New Year holiday of Rosh Hashana.

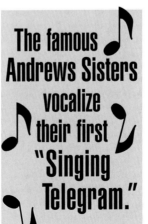

The famous Andrews Sisters vocalize their first "Singing Telegram."

32 million members make up the newly formed National Council of the Churches of Christ.

Boston's Brink's Express Company

held up by seven men who make off with $1.2 million in cash and $1.5 million in negotiables.

Organized crime reportedly outnumbering legitimate businesses in the U.S.

Senator Estes Kefauver Chairman Of Senate Crime Investigating Committee.

TOP TEN WITH A BULLET

The FBI debuts its "Ten Most Wanted Criminals" list.

THIS BEER AIN'T WHAT IT'S QUACKED UP TO BE

Dozens of drunken ducks stagger through the streets in Whitehall, New York after partaking of beer from a crashed beer truck.

A TRASHY AFFAIR

In a drive to clean up litter in Midtown New York, 4,800 additional wire trash baskets at a cost of $10 each are strategically placed by the Sanitation Department but in only five days 200 are reported stolen.

SOME DAYS YOU JUST CAN'T WIN

Italian gondoliers threaten to pull their boats out of the Venice Canals unless a red and yellow gondola advertising Coca-Cola is removed immediately as it violates the 18th Century rule that gondolas must be painted black.

THEY'D RATHER FIGHT THAN DRINK

And to add insult to injury France's Minister of Health is empowered by a National Assembly Bill to ban Coca-Cola as being injurious to health.

Teaneck, New Jersey suffers a minor set-back when, after being selected by the Army as a model American community, teenagers are banned from the town's movie theatre after they set fire to it three times.

AT THE BEHEST OF PHYSICIANS CITING INCREASED EYE INJURIES SUFFERED BY YOUNG BOYS, PHILADELPHIA BANS TOY WEAPONS INCLUDING BB GUNS.

LITTERBUGS

get the jitters as New York cops pull out all stops on giving summonses for such infractions as dropping a cigarette butt, shaking a mop or throwing garbage out the window.

WHAT A YEAR IT WAS!

SEGREGATION BARRED IN SEVERAL COLLEGES BY SUPREME COURT.

UNIVERSITY OF TEXAS

The U.S. Supreme Court rules that Heman Marion Sweatt must be admitted to the white University of Texas Law School.

DEFYING COURT RULING, UNIVERSITY OF TENNESSEE IN MEMPHIS REJECTS FIVE NEGROES.

UNIVERSITY OF OKLAHOMA

The Court grants Negro doctoral candidate G.W. McLaurin access to white facilities at University of Oklahoma.

UNIVERSITY OF VIRGINIA

Attorney Gregory Swanson enrolls in University of Virginia after courts rule the graduate courses he is seeking are not available at the state's Negro college, making him the first Negro to enter the university.

More than 1,000 Negroes attend classes with white students in 17 states with formerly segregated classrooms.

The American Red Cross announces that blood will no longer be tagged with donor's race.

A California Appellate Court holds invalid the California law restricting ownership of land by aliens on the grounds that it violates the United Nations Charter.

The Black Cat

California State Supreme Court rules that bars cannot be discriminated against because they cater to gays or lesbians thwarting attempts by the State Alcoholic Beverage Commission to shut down "**The Black Cat**," a gay bar owned by Sol Stuman.

President Truman signs bill making it easier for displaced persons to enter the United States.

The Ute Indian Tribe

of Colorado and Utah is awarded $31,700,000 by the U.S. Court of Claims as compensation for land taken from them between 1891 and 1938.

Sale of women and polygamy banned by the Communist Chinese Government.

In a U.S. Senate vote of 63-19, a constitutional amendment is passed granting women full equal rights but guaranteeing special legal protection already accorded them by law.

U.S. AIR FORCE PUTS OUT A CALL FOR WOMEN SPECIALISTS TO ENLIST FOR NON-COMBAT DUTY.

Boston University's oldest living graduate and one of the Nation's First Women Doctors, **Dr. Charlotte A. Rollins** celebrates her 101st birthday – seventy years after she is told she has only one year to live.

COFFEE, TEA AND TRO-PHEE

Beating 13 competitors, flier **Betty Haas**, of Scarsdale, New York, airline hostess and flight instructor, wins the **Powder Puff Derby** Cessna Trophy for the Daytime Event, flying from Montreal to West Palm Beach in 10 hrs. 43 min. 42 seconds.

and SPEAKING OF WOMEN WINNING

Long excluded from both the National Press and Overseas Writers clubs, newswomen finally get a break as Under Secretary of the Navy Dan Kimball throws a party for 41 White House newswomen not invited to the strictly stag annual White House Correspondents Dinner.

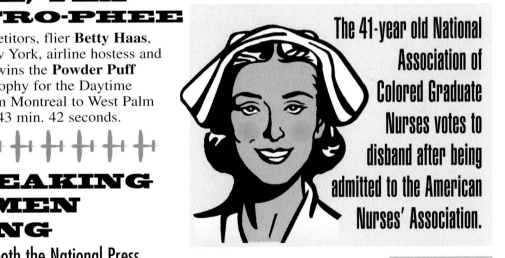

The 41-year old National Association of Colored Graduate Nurses votes to disband after being admitted to the American Nurses' Association.

INDIA GRANTS WOMEN RIGHT TO VOTE.

A WORD TO THE WISE

When asked why she stabbed her husband, a Chattanooga housewife replies that "he talks too much."

The Navy takes women reporters to war games for the first time.

1950

♪ *oh give me a home* ♪ *where* *the* ♪ *vacuum cleaner roams* ♪

In a new study, results reveal that the average woman is happiest between the ages of 25 and 45 when her role is that of a homemaker.

PROFILE OF A TYPICAL CHICAGO HOUSEWIFE

- She's 37 1/2 years old
- She's 5'4" and weighs 140 lbs.
- She's been married 18.8 years
- She has two children
- Her favorite color is blue
- She works six hours a day or less

A study conducted at an all-male college in New Jersey reveals the qualities young men want in a wife:

WELL GROOMED

GOOD CONVERSATIONALIST

SINCERE   HONEST

INTELLIGENT

ATTRACTIVE FACE & FIGURE

PLEASANT DISPOSITION

GOOD COOK
(ONLY 15% EVEN MENTIONED COOKING)

YOUR FIRST YEAR OF MARRIAGE

ARE YOU ON THE RIGHT TRACK?

A wife's check list:

- ☐ *Do you breakfast together?*
- ☐ *Can you bake?*
- ☐ *Can you provide refreshments for unexpected guests?*
- ☐ *Does your husband bring his friends home?*
- ☐ *Are meals prompt?*
- ☐ *Is he generally punctual?*
- ☐ *Is he irritable when you ask him a question?*
- ☐ *Is he interested in your friends?*
- ☐ *Does he prefer to eat out?*

Oh darlin'

I love when you talk above and below that little ol' line.

Polled college girls reveal that their ideal husband is a 6' businessman with blue eyes and annual income of $5,000. Doctors finish a distant second with lawyers a very distant third.

EGGS UP EASY

According to the U.S. Department of Agriculture, eggs should be stored with the large ends facing up.

10 ten ways to find the man of your dreams

1 Ask your married friends for introductions to eligible bachelors.

2 Be able to cook one superb dish.

3 Learn to play at least one "partner" sport or game.

4 Develop intellectual interests such as music or painting and attend concerts and art openings.

5 Enroll in an Adult Education class.

6 Find a job in a male oriented field – architecture, engineering, chemistry.

7 If you spot an attractive man, try dropping your glove.

8 If you're popular – downplay it.

9 Other women might know someone nice, so be nice to them.

10 To be an interesting person, be interested in the world around you and travel.

Good Luck and Good Hunting!

The White Plains public schools introduce a course for women in their Adult Education Program to help them understand football, boxing, tennis and other games usually understood only by men.

WHY GUYS DON'T ASK YOU OUT

✰ Sloppy Grooming
Unsuitable Clothes ✰
Bad Conversationalist
Poor Dancer ✰ Lack of Poise
Snobbish ✰ Cold ✰ Indifferent
✰ Too Sophisticated
Too Aggressive ✰
✰ Unattractive Face & Figure

YOUR TRACTOR OR MINE?

A single gentleman in Utah places an ad looking for his beloved. His requirements: Age: around 30; must own a tractor. All replies must be accompanied by a picture of her tractor.

480 MILLION OF THE 800 MILLION CHILDREN WORLDWIDE ARE UNDERNOURISHED ACCORDING TO A UNITED NATIONS REPORT.

SEND ME YOUR TIRED AND YOUR POOR...

Record number of immigrants admitted to the United States since 1929.

CENSUS BUREAU

According to latest Census Bureau reports the U.S. population is **150,520,198**. New York City is the world's second biggest city (London is first) and remains the most densely populated area anywhere.

Top ten U.S. cities

New York
Chicago
Philadelphia
Los Angeles
Detroit
Baltimore
Cleveland
St. Louis
Washington DC
Boston

UNEMPLOYMENT REACHES A 9-YEAR PEAK IN FEBRUARY.

As shoppers across the country begin hoarding sugar, nylons and tires, President Truman sternly reassures Nation that there are no threatened shortages of any essential consumer goods and that "more sugar is available than ever before."

Lots Of Maids A-Milking

Milk per cow across the land sets new record of 5,310 lbs.

The 64-year old Oleomargarine Tax repealed by Congress due to butter shortage.

U.S. FACTS ON THIS AND THAT

Median Age	30.1 years
Mental Illness	69.7 persons in every 100,000 will become mentally ill each year
Millionaires	132 in Houston, Texas out of a population of 700,000
Longevity	Nebraskans live longer than people living in any other state followed by Minnesota, the Dakotas, Iowa, Kansas and Missouri

As a cost-reducing measure, mail delivery is cut back to once a day.

The New York Times

raises its price from $.03 to $.05 a copy making it the last Manhattan daily to implement an increase.

The "New York World-Telegram and Sun" begins printing again after an 11-week strike.

SOCIAL SECURITY

3,000,000 elderly people, widows and orphans receive increased benefits under the new Social Security Act amendments raising many individual payments from $26 to $46 monthly.

WHAT A YEAR IT WAS!

The $80,000,000 Brooklyn-Battery Tunnel – longest in United States – opens in New York.

A 753-mile pipeline from Saudi Arabia to Sidon is opened by Arabian American Oil Company.

The Transcontinental Gas Pipeline Corp. brings natural gas to New York for the first time through an 1,840-mile pipeline.

Trans World Airlines, Inc. is new name of Transcontinental and Western Air, Inc.

U.S. Navy submarine travels 5,200 nautical miles in 21 days from Hong Kong to Pearl Harbor without coming up for air.

Lt. General James H. Doolittle, Jacqueline Cochran and Vice Admiral Charles E. Rosendahl receive the Harmon International Aviation Trophy from President Truman for outstanding international achievements in the arts and science of aviation.

450 members of the U.N. Secretariat move into their new internationally designed 39-story office building overlooking the East River.

1950

SOLVING THE PARKING PROBLEM

An underground garage is proposed for Los Angeles' Pershing Square.

New York City plans to use Atomic Bomb Shelters built under buildings, parks and playgrounds as underground garages during peacetime.

Oh for the good old horse and buggy days

In an effort to keep up with the growing number of people buying cars, Boston opens its first Off-Street Parking Garage, installs 3,000 additional parking meters for a total of 8,000 and adds 50 automatic traffic signs at dangerous intersections.

DAMS

Grand Coulee Dam Receives Dedication From President Truman.

Waters Flow In California's Shasta Dam For The First Time As Thousands Of People Show Up For The Formal Dedication.

Central Park's Wollman Memorial Skating Rink,
boasting almost three-quarters of an acre of skating surface, opens for skaters of all ages.

BRIDGING THE GAPS

Collapsed in 1940 due to severe winds, the new Tacoma Narrows Suspension Bridge in Tacoma, Washington opens for business.

MANHATTAN & WARD'S ISLAND
are now connected by a pedestrian bridge constructed over the Harlem River.

LET 'EM SWIM

Rockland County residents vehemently oppose the proposed Tappan Zee Bridge which would link to the state thruway.

WHAT A YEAR IT WAS!

1950

NO JOKING MATTER

In an effort to abate the country's dollar deficiency, the British Board of Trade rules that no more newspaper comics can be imported from the U.S. effecting the <u>New York Daily News and Mirror</u>.

NO LAUGHING MATTER

In an effort to maintain fairness, Britain's BBC suspends all political jokes during the general election campaign.

SNAILS & FROGS' LEGS BACK ON THE MENU

With rationing all but lifted, Londoners rejoice in being able to, once again, enjoy multi-course dinners at their favorite eateries.

120,000 former U.S. prisoners of war of Germany and Japan receive $1 for each day of imprisonment to compensate for sub-standard rations.

760 Japanese wives and children of members of U.S. Armed Forces enter the U.S. after President Truman signs bill authorizing entry.

Dresden's Mozart Girls Choir seeks sanctuary as political refugees.

Taxi-dancers chosen for their fine character as well as conversational and dancing abilities return to Berlin after being banned by the Nazis in 1933 as immoral.

The Bonn Government announces the end of rationing on all foods except sugar and German housewives can now buy all the eggs they want at $.05 each.

In a 36-35 vote, Scotland's Ayrshire County Council renames "Sex Talks" to "Biology Talks" spurring the question would "Biology Appeal" have the same draw as "Sex Appeal."

A number of Nazis teaching in Württemberg-Baden, Germany are relieved of their posts by U.S. authorities.

The Roman Catholic Church observes its Holy Year – the 25th in a series of quarter-century celebrations inaugurated more than 600 years ago by Emperor Constantine.

Hungarian Government bans virtually all Roman Catholic religious orders.

SOUTH AFRICA PASSES THE POPULATION REGISTRATION ACT WHICH CALLS FOR CLASSIFICATION OF ALL SOUTH AFRICANS AT BIRTH BY RACE.

25 British Women March In Protest Over The H-Bomb.

Almost 200 New Yorkers participate in a prayer vigil to protest the H-Bomb.

SAN FRANCISCO YOUNGSTERS RECEIVE I.D. TAGS

As part of a national program, I.D. tags are being issued carrying the name and address of the recipient with space for listing of blood type.

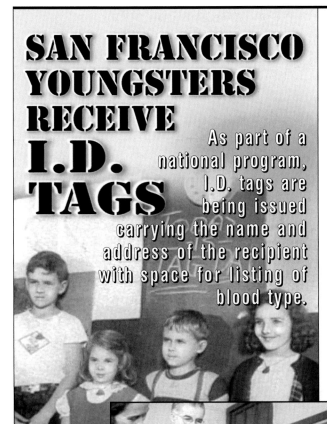

Everyone in the nation will receive a tag and in case of war or other major disasters, the tags will help first aid crews to supply prompt relief.

ACCORDING TO A UNIVERSITY OF MICHIGAN STUDY, HALF OF AMERICANS ARE ILLITERATE.

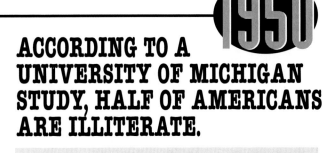

According to a nationwide survey published in the **New York Times**, more than 3,000,000 public school children are being badly educated because of ineffective programs due largely to inadequate and overcrowded classrooms and poorly-trained teachers. Also stressed is the need for early recognition of and special programs for children of high intelligence.

Enrollment in America's primary and secondary schools reaches an all-time high of 29,828,000.

Catholic School Enrollment Reaches Record High Of 3.5 Million.

We Stand By Our Story— The Stork Did It!!!

Roman Catholic Bishops object to the introduction of sex education into public schools.

Membership of boys and girls in the 4-H Clubs reaches all-time high of 1,886,214.

PARTY ANIMALS

New York's Bronx Zoo becomes a copy cat and now offers children's birthday parties much like other zoos around the country, which includes ice cream, cake and rides on animals.

DEMONSTRATION

In defiance of the school board, thousands of New York City high school students demonstrate for higher pay for their teachers.

1950

Charles Schultz's Peanuts makes its debut.

put that in your FUNK & WAGNALLS

For the first time in history, judges in the 23rd National Spelling Bee contest reverse their rulings on the correct spelling of not one, not two, not three, but four, yes count 'em, four words and reinstate the eliminated contestants. They should have used their good old Funk & Wagnalls first!

A Gallop Poll shows what the understanding of the average American is with regard to words that regularly appear in the news:

WORD	UNDERSTANDS MEANING
Flying Saucers	94%
Bookie	68%
Bipartisan Foreign Policy	26%
Point Four	5%

A flying object with red and green markings with a splash of yellow is spotted by a Santa Monica resident outside her window while a similar sighting is reported in the Santa Monica Mountains. Nearby, a pilot and his co-pilot report a brilliantly-lighted object diving under their aircraft's left wing.

HONEY, LET'S GO GET OURSELVES A PIG

Over 65,000,000 people attend over 2,200 county and state fairs held in North America spending about $250,000,000 in entertainment and goods. Price of admission: $.25 to $1.00.

some tid-bits

HOT DOG PRODUCTION	750 million pounds
POTATO CHIP PRODUCTION	320 million pounds

Best Selling Meat

#1 .... Bacon
#2 .... Ground Meat

how sweet it is!

Maple syrup is now darker and sweeter thanks to a new process which adds cane-sugar syrup.

Candies hit the market designed for eating while watching television.

LET THEM DRINK WINE!
France resumes position as #1 producer of wine.

COUNTING CALORIES
(AVERAGE DAILY CALORIC INTAKE)

WESTERN EUROPE	 2,800
UNITED STATES	 3,300

ROSES ARE NOW AVAILABLE IN 30,000 VARIETIES.

NOW YOU SEE IT, NOW YOU DON'T

Found to lack permanence, ballpoint pens are banned by the State Department.

Best Selling Christmas Toys: HOPALONG CASSIDY products

He Has A Nose For A Good Thing

The Ol' Schnoz himself JIMMY DURANTE *leads the Macy's Thanksgiving Day Parade with cowboy hero* HOPALONG CASSIDY *riding Topper and monster man* BORIS KARLOFF *on the helm of the pirate ship.*

HEY DUDE. MORE SURFIN' TIME!!
California introduces **Daylight Savings Time.**

WHAT A YEAR IT WAS!

1950

OH WELL, WE CAN HAVE ANOTHER ONE IN ONLY 350 YEARS

The Blagen Lumber Co. of White Pines, California cuts down a 350-year old, 229-foot Ponderosa Pine – largest of its kind on record.

The Society of American Foresters celebrates its 50th anniversary.

ONLY YOU CAN PREVENT FOREST FIRES

Smokey, the 4-month old black bear cub found clinging for his life to a charred tree stump in fire-ravaged Lincoln National Forest in New Mexico, becomes the United States Forest Service poster bear.

AS THE WOOD-PECKER FLIES

Long thought to be extinct, two Ivory-Billed Woodpeckers are spotted in Florida by an amateur birdwatcher and their nesting grounds are immediately converted into a 1,300-acre sanctuary.

SCOOTING RIGHT ALONG

With riders getting more than 125 miles on a gallon of gas and tires that last up to 14,000 miles, a scooter craze hits Italy.

HACKING OFF 31 INCHES

A shorter converted Chevrolet station wagon is being tested as a taxicab in New York.

HOT ROD RACING

sweeps Los Angeles.

The number of drive-in movie theatres doubles over last year reaching a total of 2,200.

LISTEN TO THIS!

The U.S. boasts 58% of the world's telephone population with Britain and Canada running second and third respectively.

ROVER DOESN'T HAVE TO REUP

The U.S. Army announces that privately owned war dogs who saw action in World War II are free of any obligation to return to active duty.

LOOKING PRETTY GOOD THERE, KIDS

The well-preserved remains of two women and four men buried 50 centuries ago are uncovered by workmen in Helwan, Egypt.

The tomb of St. Peter is discovered underneath St. Peter's Basilica in Rome.

Americans celebrate National Macaroni Week commemorating the noodle created by a young sailor who sailed with Marco Polo some 800 years ago and his beautiful Chinese paramour.

CLIMBS

Led by French climber Maurice Herzog, six men scale Annapurna, one of the highest peaks in the Himalayas.

First U.S. expedition to climb Mt. Everest reaches 18,000 feet.

NEW WORDS &

AGGRESSOR REPUBLIC
The fictitious authoritarian foe against which U.S. military personnel carry out fighting.

ARENA THEATRE
A theatre where the stage is surrounded by the audience on three sides.

BOOGIE-WOOGIE BOAT
A test ship in the Royal Air Force controlled by musical sounds emanating from another boat.

BUMPER MISSILE, ROCKET
A spacecraft that contains a booster.

CAPTIVE AUDIENCE
An audience with no additional viewing or listening options.

CATASTROPHIC COVERAGE
Personal health insurance providing abundant coverage in case of severe or prolonged sickness.

CINERAMA
Movies shot on special film stock that is projected onto larger-than-normal screens.

COLORCAST
A television show televised in Color

DEATH SAND
A potential lethal weapon made of radioactive sand.

DEMOTHBALL
When the protective casing is taken off of machinery such as airplanes or tanks.

DEFACTOIST
A person who acknowledges a de facto administration.

DIANETICS
Non-traditional therapy created by L. Ron Hubbard which helps eliminate psychosomatic ailments.

DISCIPLINED FABRIC
A special treatment given to cotton to prevent shrinkage and wrinkling.

DO
Abbreviation for an important defense order.

EAGER BEAVER
Pet name of an enormous rig that can drive through shallow water.

EXPRESSIONS

FEMINEERED
Anything created by women.

FIRE FIGHT
Close range gun combat.

FUSION BOMB
A bomb made with atomic matter such as hydrogen.

H-BOMB
Popular nickname for the hydrogen bomb.

HELL BOMB
Another name for the hydrogen bomb.

GUESTIMATE
A word used by Treasury Secretary John Snyder to calculate the number of party-goers at his daughter's wedding.

GUITAR LOOK
A female's silhouette that is broad at the hips and bosom and tapers at the waist.

K-DAY
Commencement of the Korean War.

McCARTHYISM
The often unfounded Communist accusations by Senator Joseph McCarthy against people in politics, entertainment and other professions.

MIGHTY MOUSE
Common name for the initial triumphant air-to-air missile.

PARA-RESCUE TEAM
Rescuers who reach their desired locations by jumping with parachutes from planes.

PICKLE-BARREL
A common moniker for the L-17 4-seater airplane.

RADIOLOGICAL WARFARE
Combat fought with radioactive substances.

RADIO STAR
A star with dim radiance that is detected solely by the faint radio waves it emits.

RAILPLANE
A swift loco-motive with an additional track above the cars.

RAT PACK
Rambunctious teenagers who commit crimes against innocent people after dark.

RE-EXAMINIST
A person who wants to re-examine things, especially American foreign policy.

SURFACE-TO-AIR MISSILE
An anti-aircraft missile with an automated mechanism that finds the desired point of impact.

SPACEMAN
A space explorer.

SUPERBOMB
A bomb which includes the elements tritium and/or hydrogen.

the times they are a'changing

1. ADDRESSING SOMEONE BY FIRST NAME:

Practice may be going too far when parents allow their children to address adults by their first names.

2. LOOK WHO'S WEARING TROUSERS IN THE FAMILY:

Although wearing trousers for informal occasions such as vacations, sporting events and at home is acceptable, ladies should not wear pants in the city and certain women (and you should know who you are) should never, ever entertain the thought of slipping on a pair of pants.

3. CURBING THE CURFEWS:

The days of a young woman 18 years or older having to be home before midnight are gone as the modern woman can now go for a late night snack and then be escorted home by her beau just in time to say good morning to the milkman.

4. SIT UP STRAIGHT YOUNG LADY:

Good posture seems to be a thing of the past as young girls slouch in their chairs looking more like pretzels than pretty young things.

5. THE TYPEWRITER IS MIGHTIER THAN THE PEN:

With national penmanship falling into illegibility, use of the typewriter for personal letters is not only acceptable but is actually preferable.

6. WHO IS THAT EX-HUSBAND I SAW YOU WITH?

Because so many divorced couples remain friends today, inviting them to the same party is now acceptable and no one bats an eye.

7. BUFFET DINNERS GROW IN POPULARITY:

Today's hostess who might have once lived in a big house with servants to assist in entertaining now finds the simplest way to invite friends for dinner is to serve buffet style.

8. ALAS, ALACK, CHIVALRY MAY NEVER COME BACK:

Men's hats stay on in elevators, the race is on for a seat on the bus or train and you may sit in your automobile all day if you wait for him to come 'round and open your door.

9. SMOKE GETS IN YOUR EYES:

Once considered a most unpardonable sin for a woman to smoke in public, today women can light up anytime, anywhere and inhale to their hearts content.

PASSINGS

The oldest Confederate Civil War veteran, **John Thomas Graves**, dies at the ripe old age of 108. On the other side, 101-year old Grand Army of the Republic Commander-In-Chief **Theodore A. Penland** succumbs to a heart attack.

Alcoholics Anonymous co-founder **Robert Holbrook Smith** dies at age 71.

Alice Stone Blackwell, well-known suffragist and spinster, dies at 92.

One of Geronimo's many wives, **Kate Cross Eyes** dies at age 94.

Swiss businessman **Saly Mayer**, responsible for saving a couple hundred thousand Jews from the Nazis during World War II, dies of a heart attack at age 68.

WHAT A YEAR IT WAS!

I could have danced, danced, danced all night

BUT ONLY IF YOU FOLLOW PROPER DANCE ETIQUETTE.

WOMEN:

- Wear dress shields and for heaven's sake, use a good deodorant.

- Don't get make-up on your partner's lapels.

- Grin and bear it and don't hurt his feelings even if your partner is stepping all over your feet. If you show your discontent, you look bad. Remember, it's only one dance and it won't kill you.

- If you're short, hold your elbows up high...if you're tall, lower them.

- Do not use your partner to hold you up. Stand on your own two feet.

- No chiffon ballgowns unless you are attending a formal dance.

- Don't chew gum in your partner's ear.

- Don't dance and talk at the same time. Concentrate on your dancing.

MEN:

- Use a mouthwash and a good deodorant.

- Do not use smelly hair tonics.

- Make sure your hands are dry (use your handkerchief).

- Never leave a girl alone on the dance floor – escort her back to her chair.

- If you are on a date, it is exceptionally rude to leave her alone while you dance with someone else.

- If she's a poor dancer, don't embarrass her by getting too fancy.

- Don't teach your partner on the dance floor or offer helpful hints.

- Don't fall apart if either of you makes a mistake. Just say you're sorry.

- Be gracious when someone cuts in.

- Don't hike up her dress in the back.

GRAB YOUR PARTNER AND GIVE HER A TWIRL

The Haylofters play at the second annual Square Dance Jamboree in Waterbury, Connecticut's Municipal Stadium

Arthur Murray's
LIST OF BEST MALE NON-PROFESSIONAL DANCERS

Conrad Hilton

Lowell Thomas

Philip Wylie

Robert Montgomery

Walter Winchell

Bert Parks

"Now, sir, are you ready for the next question about metals?"

CONTESTANTS

John Reed King, Quiz Master on Give and Take, C.B.S.

QUESTION What is our cheapest metal and what does it cost per pound—5¢, 19¢, 75¢?

ANSWER *Steel is our cheapest metal.* And Steel is sold at an average price of *less than 5¢ a pound*, f.o.b. the mills, by America's more than 200 steel companies. That's why steel is so widely used.

Steel works for EVERYONE

See how Steel's average price compares with that of other metals.
Recent prices have been ranging like this:

Steel	.5¢ lb.	Aluminum	17¢ lb.
Zinc	10¢ lb.	Copper	19¢ lb.
Lead	12¢ lb.	Antimony	25¢ lb.
	Tin	75¢ lb.	

AMERICAN IRON AND STEEL INSTITUTE, 350 FIFTH AVENUE, NEW YORK 1, N. Y.

BUSINESS

Your **paycheck is a bit smaller** as U.S. **withholding rates go up** from 15% to 18%.

Legal **minimum wage raised** to $.75 per hour.

The Spanish island of *Majorca* becomes the first *Club Med* location.

Famous Birth
Steve Wozniak

A Juicy Budget

Minute Maid Orange Juice has an advertising budget of around $2,000,000 to promote its frozen concentrated orange juice.

1950
UNION NEWS

400,000 WORKERS IN SIX STATES PARTICIPATE IN SOFT-COAL STRIKE

Refusing To Comply With A Court Order 370,000 Miners Defy John L. Lewis' Command To Return To Work

COAL MINERS STRIKE ENDS AFTER LENGTHY NEGOTIATIONS

John L. Lewis

General Motors signs a 5-year contract for pay and pension increases.

Chrysler's 100-day strike ends after agreement is reached on a pension and social security insurance benefits.

The constitutionality of the non-Communist affidavit of the Taft-Hartley labor management relations law is upheld by the U.S. Supreme Court.

An agreement is signed between Bethlehem Steel and U.S. Steel calling for a 10% average wage increase.

American Telephone and Telegraph subsidiaries in 42 states are hit by a strike by 33,000 members of the C.I.O. Communications Workers of America. After 25 hours of bargaining an agreement is reached and phone service is no longer disrupted.

An increase of $7.50 a week is the demand of the 250 striking A.F.L. teletype operators of the United Press.

Locomotive Firemen go on strike against four U.S. railroads demanding a second fireman on multiple-unit diesel electric engines. Strike goes to arbitration.

Four major western railroads suspend operations as the Switchmens Union of North America strike for shorter hours and more pay.

Brotherhood of Railroad Trainmen call for wildcat strike against 15 Chicago railroads.

Truman orders railroads seized to avoid nationwide strike. Strike by 300,000 workers called off following threat of seizure.

Wage dispute settled between railroad labor unions and management with a 3-year contract calling for substantial wage increases including cost of living increases. Brotherhood of Locomotive Engineers reject proposed settlement.

WHAT A YEAR IT WAS!

GIVE-

The easiest-writing portable ever built!

THE NEW ROYAL

More "big-machine" features than any other portable

Twice as much quick magic in setting margins. The new Royal has both right and left hand "Magic" Margins! Position, press, margin set! As easy as turning on a light switch! A Royal exclusive!

Your fingers get away like a rabbit with the new Speed-King Keyboard and high speed key action. Office typewriter specifications. Finger-Flow keys of non-glare plastic. Truly, this is the world's fastest portable!

It's a big, husky typewriter! New features include larger cylinder knobs—newly designed Finger Comfort Controls. And there's greater visibility in setting tab stops. It also has a new revolutionary Contour Case.

PLUS Picture Window writing line visibility, new Paper Lock Scale for easy centering, spacing, and tab arrangements. Plus exclusive "Touch Control." Long writing line—a full 9 inches.

ROYAL-World's No.1 Portable Typewriter

TRULY THE STANDARD TYPEWRITER IN PORTABLE SIZE. ASK YOUR DEALER ABOUT TERMS!

"Magic" and "Touch Control" are registered trade-marks of Royal Typewriter Company, Inc.

LET'S SEE YOU TALK YOURSELVES OUT OF THIS ONE, SLICK

The U.S. Justice Department files an antitrust suit against seven West Coast oil companies, including Standard Oil Co. of California, charging them with monopoly and price-fixing.

Preston Tucker and seven of his associates are found not guilty of mail fraud and conspiracy stemming from the development of a rear-engine car which they began working on after World War II.

R.H. Macy & Co. defies fair trade laws and slashes prices on toasters and other small appliances.

NOTHING TO SNEEZE AT

Two American companies are charged with false and misleading advertising in their antihistamine cold tablets ads.

Ferdinand Porsche opens a factory in Stuttgart, Germany.

Chrysler Corporation celebrates its 25th anniversary.

Oldsmobile produces its 1,000,000th Hydra-matic equipped vehicle.

General Electric unveils an electric computer which allows automobile plant supervisors to uncover defective parts within minutes vs. the hours it previously took to track down a problem.

Let's See, Bread, Butter, Cheese And Oh, Yes, This Cute Little Car

Jumping on the one-stop shop bandwagon, Kings Supermarket in Plainfield, New Jersey offers a Hillman Minx convertible for $1,745.

Passings

Automobile pioneer and Oldsmobile creator **Ransom Eli Olds**, who began his career working on carriages, dies at age 86.

WHAT A YEAR IT WAS!

ONLY HER HAIRDRESSER WILL KNOW FOR SURE

Clairol, Inc. introduces a new formula which bleaches, shampoos and tints all in one application which will save ladies time and money.

Brooklynite **Beatrice Rosenberg** who started as a hat clerk in 1918 becomes R.H. Macy & Co.'s first woman vice president in the company's 92-year history.

Women are employed in every major industry in the United States and represent nine out of every ten workers in some apparel industries.

THE NEW YORKER MAGAZINE CELEBRATES **25** YEARS OF PUBLISHING.

— Getting On Track —

Taking up a full square block, the $24,000,000 New York Port Authority Bus Terminal is ready to commence operations by year-end and is equipped to service around 136,000 passengers a day.

Paying With Plastic
(a new concept)

New York-based **DINERS CLUB** introduces a new plastic charge for use as a cash substitute when paying for meals in 27 participating restaurants.

* **American Express** celebrates its 100th anniversary.

* **New York's Chemical Bank & Trust Company** transports $5,000,000,000 in securities—the most valuable shipment in U.S. history.

* **Air Canada** begins service between Montreal and New York's La Guardia airport.

* **Boston's Filene's Department Store** installs special coin vending machines in a Greyhound bus terminal to dispense a select group of consumer items.

1950 this was the price that was

A Nickel Will Get You:
Cola, Cough Drops, Head of Lettuce, Jujyfruits, Junior Mints, Kool-Aid, Life Savers, *New York Times*, Shoe Laces, Staten Island Ferry

FOOD

Baked Beans at Howard Johnson's . . .	$ .40
Bread, 1 lb.	.14
Butter, 1 lb.	.68
Candy Bar	.10
Carrots, lb.	.05
Chinese Food, take-out	1.35
Coffee, 1 lb.	.75
Corn on the Cob, 2 ears	.19

Cottage Cheese, pt.	$ .18
Cracker Jack, 2 boxes	.09
Eggs, 1 dz.	.49
Fritos	.19
Ice Cream Soda	.25
Jack Cheese, 1 lb.	.45
Mayonnaise, pt.	.37
Milk, qt.	.20
Oranges, 1 lb.	.04

MORE FOOD

Peanut Butter, 15 oz.	$ .37
Pecans, 1 lb.	.29
Tomatoes, 1 lb.	.10
Whitman's Sampler, 1 lb.	2.00

FOR HIM

After Shave, 12 oz.	$ .98
Bow Tie	1.00
Briefs	.80
Denim Jeans, boys	2.29
Pipe	3.50
Wallet	7.50
Brooks Bros. Flannel Suit	105.00
Flannel Trousers	20.00
Oxford Cloth Shirt	4.25

Hat	$ 7.50-20.00
Shoes	9.95-15.95
Van Cleef & Arpels gold & sapphire cuff links	390.00

FOR HER

Chanel Perfume, 2 oz.	$ 32.50
Dusting Powder	1.50
Girdle	7.50-15.00
Designer Dress	135.00
Home Permanent Kit	2.00
Mascara	2.50
Pedal Pushers	2.98
Shoes	7.95-18.95
Sweater, cashmere	10.00-20.00
Tiffany diamond & sapphire earrings	2,200.00

TRANSPORTATION

Airfare, LA to NY . . . . . $ 75.00-88.00 one-way
Greyhound Bus, NY to SF   49.80 one-way
Gasoline, gallon 23
Motor oil, quart 45
Jaguar XK120 . . . . 3,945.00
MG Roadster 1,850.00
Streetcar fare, St. Louis 15

Housing

5th Avenue, NY, 5 room apt . $ 367/month
Greenwich, CT, 4 br. house 42,500
Levittown, NY, 2 br. house 7,990
Malibu, CA, 2 br. house 21,500
San Francisco, CA, 1 br. apt . . . 62/month
Santa Monica, CA, 1 br. apt . . . 75/month

ENTERTAINMENT

Ballet Theatre . . . . $ 3.00 top
Circus 1.50-6.00
Dinner at Copacabana, NYC . . 2.50
Dinner at Maxim's, Paris 10.00
Fair, entrance fee 25-1.00
Fairmont Hotel, NYC, suite . . 61.00
Henry Fonda on Broadway,
    in "Mister Roberts" 1.20-4.80
Hotel, Atlantic Beach 2.00
Monopoly board game 4.00
Movie 55
Paperback Book 25
National Symphony Orchestra,
    season tickets 67.00

FOR THE HOME

Alarm Clock, electric . . . . . . $ 4.50
Coffeemaker, automatic 24.95
Dishwasher, portable 169.50
Furniture Set, 11 pieces . . . 198.00
Georg Jensen Salad Bowl . . 24.50
Hopalong Cassidy Radio . . . 16.95
Lightbulb, 100 watt. 21
Paint, gallon. 4.69
Pillow. 9.95
Refrigerator. 189.95
Scale 6.95-9.95
Scotch Tape 25
Stapler 2.45
Steuben Glasses, set of 12 . . 100.00
Toaster, automatic 21.50
TV Console, 165 sq. in. . . . 399.95

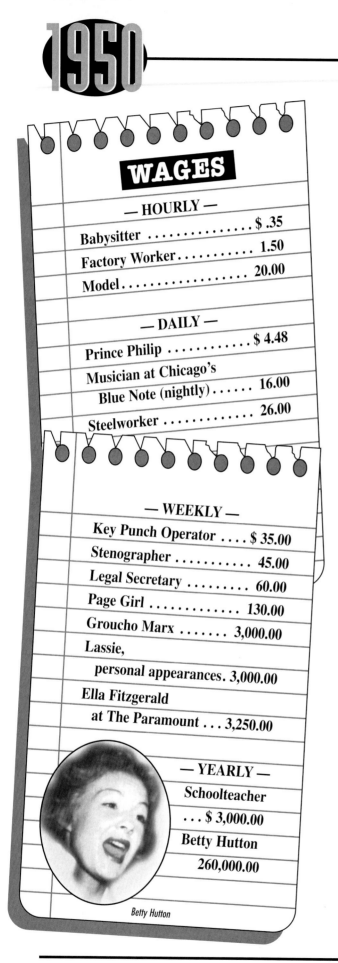

WAGES

— HOURLY —

Babysitter . . . . $ .35
Factory Worker 1.50
Model 20.00

— DAILY —

Prince Philip . . . . $ 4.48
Musician at Chicago's
Blue Note (nightly) 16.00
Steelworker 26.00

— WEEKLY —

Key Punch Operator . . . . $ 35.00
Stenographer 45.00
Legal Secretary 60.00
Page Girl 130.00
Groucho Marx 3,000.00
Lassie,
    personal appearances. 3,000.00
Ella Fitzgerald
    at The Paramount . . . 3,250.00

— YEARLY —

Schoolteacher
. . . $ 3,000.00
Betty Hutton
    260,000.00

Betty Hutton

SCIENCE & MEDICINE

The Dawning Of The
Atomic Age

*"**Radioactive poisoning of the atmosphere** and hence annihilation of any life on earth has been brought within the range of technical possibilities...In the end, there beckons more and more clearly general annihilation..."*

—Albert Einstein

January

President Truman Authorizes The Atomic Energy Commission To Develop The Hydrogen Bomb (H-Bomb)

E.I. du Pont de Nemours Wins The Contract To Find A 200,000 Acre Site On Which To Build And Run A Plant To Produce The H-Bomb

August

The First H-Bomb Is Detonated In The South Pacific Obliterating A Small Island

WHAT A YEAR IT WAS!

Then...Kiss Your Tush Goodbye!

In an effort to calm A-Bomb jitters, Washington issues a pamphlet called **Survival Under Atomic Attack** with some of the following suggestions if The Bomb drops:

A. If An Air Raid Warning Sounds

- Turn off gas and electricity

- Close all doors, windows

- Draw curtains

- Go to the basement

- Cover neck, head and arms to protect against flying glass, heat and radiation

B. If Bomb Falls Without Advance Warning

- Turn away from the flash, fall flat, close your eyes, cover head and arms against flash burns. Crawl under a bed, desk or behind a sofa

- If outdoors, stand as close to a building or tree as you can to protect against falling debris

C. After All-Clear Signal Sounds

- Cover mouth and nose with handkerchief to protect against radioactive dust

- Nail blinds over broken windows

- Change clothes, scrub body, hair and finger-nails with plenty of soap to get off radioactive particles

- DON'T use telephone, water, eat, drink or touch anything that might be contaminated

You Mean I Don't Have To Kiss My Tush Goodbye?

According to a California scientist if an A-Bomb falls relax and hold your breath as running around increases the supply of oxygen to the body which intensifies the effects of the deadly radioactive rays.

Following An A-Bomb Attack,

a solution of one level teaspoon of table salt and one-half teaspoon of baking soda taken orally is recommended as an easy and practical way to treat shock.

And Now For The Good News About That Can Of Sardines

Packaged or canned food will probably be safe to eat after the bomb blast and unprotected foods can be eaten if the outer contaminated layers are removed.

The world's most powerful atom smasher, the new **SYNCHRO-CYCLOTRON**, begins operating at Irvington-on-Hudson, New York under the leadership of New York's Columbia University.

A 200-ton atom smasher, the second largest in the world, begins tests at University of Chicago under the guidance of Nobel-winning physicist **DR. ENRICO FERMI.**

NOT TO BE TAKEN LIGHTLY

Britain develops a machine that causes atomic particles to travel at close to the speed of light—186,000 miles per second.

In the first practical use of an atom smasher, **UPJOHN PHARMACEUTICAL** announces the sterilization of antibiotics using a 2-million volt electron accelerator.

Monsieur, Ees That A Bomb In Your Pocket?

Vaucluse, a small town in the South of France, passes an ordinance banning the bearing or use of atomic or hydrogen bombs within city limits.

For Your Eyes Only

The University of Pittsburgh announces the development of two kinds of glass that will protect eyes against atomic rays.

A Do-It-Yourself Radioactive Kit

New York's 47th annual American Toy Fair unveils an authentic little atomic energy laboratory for a low price of $42.50 complete with three radioactive ore samples, a geiger counter and a spinthariscope.

Head Of The Atomic Energy Commission Voices Concern That The U.S. Will Be Facing A Shortage Of Atomic Research Scientists.

The Brookhaven National Laboratory Is The Site Of The Largest And Most Powerful Nuclear Reactor Designed For Research Purposes Only.

Permission To Build The First Non-Governmental Reactor In The United States Is Granted To North Carolina State College In Raleigh, North Carolina By The Atomic Energy Commission.

The White House Announces The Development Of Atomic Artillery Shells And Warheads For Guided Missiles.

Editor Of **THE SATURDAY REVIEW OF LITERATURE**, Norman Cousins, Expresses His Fear That The World Is Engaged In A Game Of Atomic Russian Roulette.

THE ATOMIC ENERGY COMMISSION ANNOUNCES THE FIRST PRACTICAL METHOD FOR CONVERTING ATOMIC ENERGY INTO ELECTRICITY WITHOUT THE USE OF BOILERS OR DYNAMOS HAS BEEN DISCOVERED BY CHICAGO SCIENTISTS.

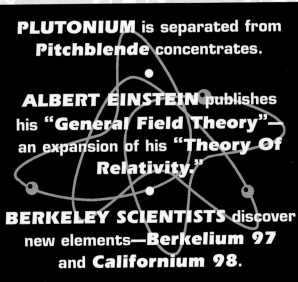

PLUTONIUM is separated from **Pitchblende** concentrates.

ALBERT EINSTEIN publishes his *"General Field Theory"*— an expansion of his *"Theory Of Relativity."*

BERKELEY SCIENTISTS discover new elements—**Berkelium 97** and **Californium 98.**

A MOOOVING EXPERIENCE

First Embryo Successfully Implanted In Cattle.

IT'S FOR SOME UTTER REASON

Variations In The Way Milk Tastes Should Not Be Blamed On Bessie As Influences Such As Sunlight Or Foods With Strong Odors Can Effect A Change In Flavor.

THE CASE OF THE VANISHING CHICK

The Aransas National Wildlife Refuge In Texas Announces The Disappearance Of The First Rare Whooping Crane Born In Captivity.

Contrary To Popular Belief, Wool Grows Faster On Sheep In The Summer And Early Fall.

THEY DRINK LIKE FISH

Two University Of Chicago Zoologists Confirm That When Fish Are Thirsty They Drink Water.

IN SEARCH OF THE MONSTER

A Danish team of scientists set sail from England to try their luck at finding sea monsters. Meanwhile, in Scotland, there is another sighting of the evasive LOCH NESS MONSTER.

START FILLING THOSE WATER BOTTLES

Swedish professor of oceanography Dr. Hans Pettersson warns that the water shortages currently being experienced in New York, and indeed throughout the world, are just the tip of the water berg and he predicts that the planet will be waterless in a few thousand million years.

Under the joint auspices of Scripps Institute of Oceanography and the electronics laboratory of the U.S. Navy, 30 scientists and 85 crew members complete a monumental 29,000-mile study of the Pacific ocean bottom from Cape Mendocino, California to Wake, Kwajalein.

Don't Stow Those Leftover Spuds

Cooked potatoes used the next day lose from a third to one-half of their vitamin C according to tests conducted at the Minnesota Experiment Station Show.

As Corny As It May Sound

In an attempt to combat hunger, the first shipment of hybrid corn is sent to India.

Experiments conducted at Cornell University in Ithaca, New York reveal that cheese may be free of bacteria by pasteurizing it with radio waves after the cheese has aged.

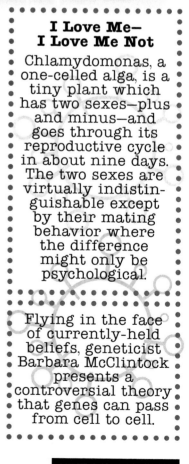

I Love Me— I Love Me Not

Chlamydomonas, a one-celled alga, is a tiny plant which has two sexes—plus and minus—and goes through its reproductive cycle in about nine days. The two sexes are virtually indistinguishable except by their mating behavior where the difference might only be psychological.

Flying in the face of currently-held beliefs, geneticist Barbara McClintock presents a controversial theory that genes can pass from cell to cell.

By testing a single ounce of wood from an Egyptian mummy's casket, a new method for dating archaeological discoveries called "Atomic Calendar" is used by scientists at the University of Chicago Institute for Nuclear Studies to calculate the age of the deceased to be around 4,750 years old.

1,400-year old Mogollon Indian mummies are discovered near Reserve, New Mexico.

Here's Something To Chew Over

Mrs. Otis Strand of Woodman, Wisconsin finds a 6 ½ pound prehistoric mastodon molar uncovered on her dad's farm during recent floods.

CONGRESS PASSES A BILL creating the **National Science Foundation** which will make $15,000,000 available each year to researchers in basic science.

THE UNIVAC I, first computer on the open market, is built by engineers John Mauchly and John Eckert.

TRANSISTORS that will be activated by light rather than electric current are in development at Bell Telephone Laboratories.

CITING SOVIET RESEARCH into this deadly form of weaponry, the development of nerve gases is revealed by the Army Chemical Corps Chief General Anthony McAuliffe.

ENGLISH is becoming the language of choice for more than half of the world's scientific papers—the balance written in French, German, Russian or Italian.

A Half Brain Idea

Harry Harlow, professor of psychology at the University of Wisconsin, concludes that sometimes half a brain may be better than one according to tests conducted on monkeys. He discovers that a large amount of brain tissue can be destroyed without negatively impacting on the monkey's intellectual abilities.

WHAT A YEAR IT WAS!

1950

The Plane Truth

The world's fastest bomber, the **Boeing B-47 A**, with air speed capability of 600 m.p.h., can carry over 20,000 pounds of bombs or an atomic bomb.

British jet plane **The Hawker** makes its flying debut.

A new oxygen-bearing helmet designed to protect pilots bailing out at 400 m.p.h. or faster is developed by the U.S. Air Force.

Canada's **Avro** carrier arrives in New York after a record 59-minute, 56-second flight marking the first international jet transport in North America.

Striving for supremacy in jet-powered military aircraft, Britain unveils its **Gloster Interceptor** fighter.

Record parachute jump from 42,449 feet is made by **Captain R.V. Wheeler** at Holloman Air Force Base in New Mexico.

A New York University research balloon set adrift at Holloman Air Force Base drifts 7,000 miles to Myrdal, Norway.

Captain **Charles "Chuck" Yeager's Bell X-1** which broke the sound barrier in 1948 is turned over to the Smithsonian Institution to become part of its historic 100-plane collection.

The Big Bazooka, a U.S. anti-tank weapon, goes into military use in Korea.

Army's first attempt to launch a guided missile fails.

The Defense Department announces the successful testing of the first air-to-air rocket for use in aerial combat.

A rocket fired from the deck of the U.S.S. Norton Sound rises 106.4 miles setting a new record for single-stage American rockets.

Soaring 107 miles into the stratosphere, the Navy sets a new record with its **Viking** rocket, launched at the White Sands, New Mexico proving grounds.

It's All In The Stars Dear Brutus

Light from an exploding star heading to earth over 50 million years ago is recorded with the 200-inch Hale telescope on Palomar Mountain, the furthest distance a stellar explosion has ever been documented.

A NEW ESTIMATE FOR THE SPEED OF LIGHT is 186,280 miles per second according to Stanford University physicists.

Hello? Is Anybody Out There?

In a Harvard astronomical survey of the Big Dipper region of the northern sky 1,500 new universes are discovered with millions more yet to be uncovered.

A Laughing Matter

It is confirmed that there are traces of nitrous oxide (laughing gas) in the atmosphere.

It's Not The Size That Counts

Using the Hale telescope, Dr. Gerard P. Kuiper of the University of Chicago discovers that the 3,600-mile diameter of Pluto is actually less than previously thought.

Starry, Starry, Starry Night

Using observatories in England and South Africa, Yale Observatory ends a 23-year research project to catalog over 128,000 stars positioned 30 degrees south of the celestial equator and 30 degrees north.

Look Up In The Sky

It's A....

According to a report called Psychological Analysis of Reports of Unidentified Aerial Objects (flying saucers), following is a list of what you could be looking at:

**Airplanes
Birds
Kites
Venus
Fireflies
Weather Balloons
Fireballs
Parachute & Pistol Flares
Meteors
Comets**

Blue Skies Smiling At You

The color of the sky on a typical day on Mars is deep blue according to the Royal Astronomical Society in Dublin.

Or It Could Be A Flying Saucer!

WHEN YOU MOTOR to Natchez, Miss., you'll see some of the most beautiful homes and gardens in the entire South. This mansion, Stanton Hall, was built in 1856, and furnished with a whole shipload of exquisite mantels, chandeliers and mirrors from France and Spain.

There's no place like America for motoring! And never before has motoring been as much fun as it is with today's great new cars—the greatest cars America has ever known!

To help keep your new car running like new, use Gulfpride —the only motor oil that is *Alchlor-processed.*

The Alchlor process is an *extra* refining step. It makes Gulfpride *extra* pure and *extra* efficient—makes it, as thousands of motorists will tell you, *the world's finest motor oil!*

P. S. For top quality and top value, get famous Gulf Tires and Gulf Batteries. Ask your Gulf dealer about 'em—*today!*

Keep your new car new — use

Gulfpride

the world's finest motor oil!

Gulf Oil Corporation · Gulf Refining Company

KEEP THOSE ASPIRINS HANDY

The Average American Experiences 50 Headaches A Year With The Total Number Of Headaches Up Around 7 1/2 Billion.

WHAT A PAIN IN THE NECK

Backaches Rank As The Nation's No. 2 Source Of Pain.

11,000 Students Are Enrolled In U.S. Dental Schools.

The Chiropractic Profession Urges Americans To "Stand Tall, Sit Tall And Walk Tall" During Correct Posture Week.

The "New York Times" Publishes A Report Conducted By The United Nations Educational, Scientific And Cultural Organization Which Indicates There Is No Scientific Evidence That One Race Is Superior To Another.

Chronic Diarrhea May Have Its Origins In Nervous Disorders.

CRACKING THROUGH TRADITIONAL MEDICAL BARRIERS

The United States has 20,000 licensed chiropractors practicing in all states excluding Louisiana, Massachusetts, Mississippi and New York.

THERE IS DEFINITELY A DOCTOR IN THE HOUSE

According to the American Medical Association the United States has more doctors than any other country (except Israel) in the world followed by England, Denmark, Canada and New Zealand.

HE MAKES HOUSE CALLS

Dr. Dean Sherwood Luce Of Canton, Massachusetts Is Honored As Family Doctor Of The Year By The American Medical Association.

One In Every 100 Americans Have Pigeon-Toed Feet.

IS THERE A WOMAN DOCTOR IN THE HOUSE?

Dr. Helen B. Tausig is the first female admitted to the Association of American Physicians.

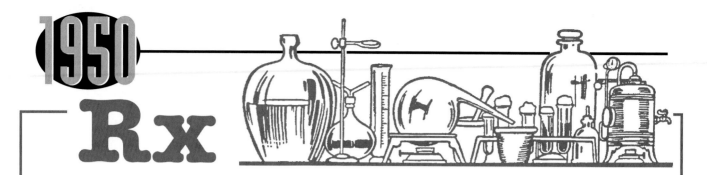

1950

Rx

- For Patients Suffering From Overactive Thyroid Problems Radioactive Iodine Is An Effective Means Of Treatment.

- Antihistamines Grow In Popularity As A Home Remedy For Allergy And Cold Symptoms.

- Daily Doses Of Vitamin B-12 Are Having A Positive Result In Treating Under-Nourished Children.

- Antibiotics Are The Leading Drugs Used In The Treatment Of A Variety Of Diseases.

- People Suffering From Peptic Ulcers May Be Able To Avoid Surgery By Receiving Treatment With A New Ulcer Drug Called Banthine According To Testing Currently Being Done.

- Cortisone Found Effective In Treating Certain Forms Of Arthritis.

- Dr. Albert B. Sabin Of The Children's Hospital Research Foundation Of Cincinnati Discovers An Anti-Polio Substance In Mother's Milk.

- Methadone Is Used As A Substitute For Narcotics.

- Terramycin Is A Bacteria-Killing Drug.

- Hailed As The Greatest Breakthrough In Antibiotics Since The Discovery Of Penicillin In 1928, Elizabeth L. Hazel And Rachel Brown Announce Their Discovery Of Nystatin, A Derivative Of The Streptomycin Group, As Being The First Safe Fungicide.

DON'T MONKEY AROUND ON THIS ONE

Vitamin B1 Deficiency May Cause Severe Brain Damage Confirms Tests Conducted On Monkeys.

MUMS THE WORD ON MUMPS

Lederle Laboratories Announce The Production Of A Preventive Vaccine Against Mumps.

Horses get almost instant relief of charley horse pain with injections of vitamins B and C according to the American Veterinary Medical Association.

TB OR NOT TB

The Rockefeller Institute of Medical Research is developing a new blood test which can detect the presence of TB.

Venereal disease is wiped out in Haiti through penicillin.

WHAT A YEAR IT WAS!

the CANCER front

⭐ According To A Report Published In The British Medical Journal Smoking Is A Very Important Element In Causing Lung Cancer.

⭐ Growing Evidence Seems To Indicate That There Is A Direct Link Between Lung Cancer And Cigarette Smoking According To Dr. Evarts A. Graham Of Washington University In St. Louis.

⭐ Earmarked For The Treatment Of Cancer Patients, New York's Roosevelt Hospital Gets $1,000,000 Worth Of Radium (50 Grams), The Largest Amount Ever Stored In A Single Apparatus, Giving The Hospital The Most Powerful Radium-Beam Machine In The World.

⭐ Florida Reports A Skin Cancer Rate Of Three To Four Times Higher Than The Rest Of The Country, Found Predominantly Among Farmers, Fishermen, Outdoor Laborers And Pitch Workers.

⭐ Loose Cells From The Stomach Lining Can Be Captured By A Silk Brush Attached To A 4-Inch Balloon As An Aid In Detecting Stomach Cancer.

⭐ Dr. George Papanicolaou Of New York Hospital-Cornell Medical Center Receives A Lasker Award From The American Public Health Association For His Development Of The Smear Test Used To Detect Cervical Cancer.

GET OUT THOSE SHORT SLEEVE SHIRTS

In order to quickly identify blood types in case of an A-Bomb attack, the Chicago Medical Civil Defense Committee approves voluntary tattooing of blood types below the armpit.

Cases of **THE PLAGUE**, or as it was known in medieval times the "**BLACK DEATH**," are reported in New Mexico.

Acquitted of the mercy killing of a cancer patient, **DR. HERMANN SANDER** of Candia, New Hampshire is back in his office treating patients.

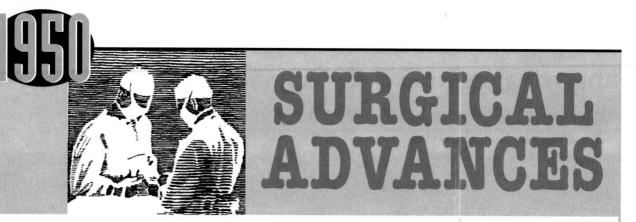

SURGICAL ADVANCES

Surgery for the removal of gallstones may become a thing of the past with the use of high frequency sound waves currently being tested as a means for breaking up the stones.

MUSIC THAT DOTH SOOTH THE SAVAGE NERVES

Soft, soothing music is finding its way into Duke University and University of Chicago operating rooms as a means of keeping patients calm.

The Mayo Clinic's Reginald G. Bickford and Albert Faulconer, Jr. invent an electronic device for controlling the depth of anesthesia during operations.

Dr. Charles Bailly reports the discovery of a heart-lung device to revive the clinically dead.

A man pronounced dead twice during surgery is brought back to life through manual heart massage.

Chicago Drs. Richard Lawler and James West successfully transplant a kidney in a human being.

WHAT PRICE SUCCESS?

TWO OUT OF EVERY FIVE of the 55 business leaders under the age of 50 examined by two Chicago doctors show a low level of blood sugar and only three are in good health. Poor conditions range from high blood pressure to being overweight to heart conditions.

Paris Is The Location Of The First International Congress Of Cardiology Which 1,200 Doctors Attend.

NOBEL PRIZES

MEDICINE & PHYSIOLOGY
Philip S. Hench (U.S.A.)
and
Edward C. Kendall (U.S.A.)
and
Tadeus Reichstein
(Switzerland)

PHYSICS
Cecil F. Powell
(Great Britain)

CHEMISTRY
Otto P.H. Diels
(Germany)
and
Kurt Alder
(Germany)

PSYCHIATRY

According to **Dr. Richard L. Jenkins**, Chief of Research at the Veterans Administration Psychiatry and Neurology Division, a contributing factor to schizophrenia is frustration in family or inter-personal relationships where the patient fails to achieve satisfaction.

Researchers at the University of Pennsylvania find obesity seems to have its roots in stress, frustration and lack of love, and obese people are usually non-aggressive and dependent on outside love and approval.

A Personality Test Discloses Neurotic People Have More Dental Decay Than Their Well-Adjusted Counterparts.

I Forgot Exactly What I Was Depressed About

Extensive use of electroshock therapy for mental disorders relieves depression but causes memory loss.

A researcher at the Yale University School of Medicine believes normal people are better at lying than neurotics, demonstrating greater skills in avoiding answering questions while under the influence of hypnotic drugs called truth serums.

People With A Superiority Complex Usually Have An Inferiority Complex As Well With One Compensating For The Other According To Dr. Harrington V. Ingham Of The University Of California At Los Angeles.

Anxiety is the result of feeling helpless and paralyzed to take action according to studies conducted at University of California Medical School and takes some of the following physical forms:

- Rapid Pulse
- Blushing Or Sweating
- Restlessness
- Rapid, Shallow Breathing
- Deep Sighs
- High-Pitched, Shrill Or Loud Voice
- Inappropriate Laughter

MORNING TYPES:
Reach Peak Performance Early In The Day

EVENING TYPES:
Raring To Go Late In The Day And Hate Getting Up In The Morning

- Temple University's Department of Psychiatry publishes list of common emotions that are connected to illness which include need for love, approval and recognition, fear and worry, guilt, ambition and envy.

- 10,000 more psychiatrists are currently needed in the United States to treat the one out of ten people suffering from mental disorders a Yale University study reveals.

- A self-accepting person is more apt not to harbor racial prejudice than someone who is unhappy with himself.

IS THAT AN ITCH YOU'RE SCRATCHING OR ARE YOU WISHING I WAS OUT OF HERE?

A five-year study conducted at the New York Academy of Sciences concludes one's body language is quite revealing as every posture has specific meaning.

HEY HONEY, WHERE DID YOU PUT MY OTHER BLUE SOCK?

All geniuses are not a little mad but indeed appear to be mentally well-balanced proclaims a study of over 250 gifted people ranging from poets and painters to scientists, conducted by an Austrian psychiatrist.

WOMEN

In an article appearing in **The Journal Of The American Medical Association**, doctors suspect that about three out of every four women are frigid and are not being sexually satisfied for some of the following reasons:

1. **Fear of punishment for violating society's taboos on sex.**

2. **Confusion about loving feelings.**

3. **Unconscious resentment of men for the suffering they've caused.**

A new film on **Breast Self-Examination** produced jointly by the **American Cancer Society** and the **National Cancer Institute of the United States Public Health Service** attracts a great deal of attention at the 99th convention of the **American Medical Association**.

YES, *BUT WILL I GROW A BEARD?*

According to an article published in **The Journal Of The American Medical Association,** tests conducted at Bellevue Hospital reveal that women experience relief from menstrual pain by taking small amounts of the male hormone methyltestosterone by mouth for six days before ovulation.

A paper published in "Science Service" claims **men are the weaker sex** having much more difficulty in handling **aging**, greater incidences of **emotional** and fatal **physical illnesses** and higher rates of **alcoholism, delinquency** and **suicide**.

Licorice, a component in an over-the-counter home remedy women use during their cycle, is found to contain traces of the female hormone estrogen.

Sleepy Time Gal

A recently published book on the subject of sleep reveals women need an hour more sleep than men; the divorce rate is lower among couples who sleep in double beds; three men snore for every one woman (whistle softly or drop a piece of soap in his mouth to get him to stop snoring).

If you can't get him to stop snoring, *Miltown* is a popular tranquilizer.

You Gotta Laugh A Little, You Gotta Cry A Little

Recent studies show women can feel greater happiness than men but also can feel greater sadness.

What?? And Let My Gray Hair Show?

Certain beauty aids such as hair dyes, hair treatments, shampoos and permanent wave lotions may be responsible for skin disorders some women have developed.

Evidence is uncovered that women who use metal curlers to set their hair or wear it in tight braids may develop bald spots above their ears.

WHAT A YEAR IT WAS!

DON'T TOUCH THAT CORD

According to Dutch research, cutting the umbilical cord ten to fifteen minutes after birth greatly benefits the newborn infant.

JUST BABY AND ME AND NURSIE MAKES THREE

30 American hospitals offer facilities for mothers to keep their newborn babies in the room with them.

Breast feeding vs. cow's milk is the subject of Dr. Stuart Shelton Stevenson's lecture before the American Dietetic Association where, although he endorses breast-feeding (vitamin C), he also makes a case for the merits of cow's milk (more calcium).

According to a new study, children of younger mothers (20-25) can expect to live up to 10 to 15 years longer than children of older mothers (40).

Research reveals about 10% of all marriages in America and Great Britain are childless due to one of the partners being unable to reproduce.

The electrohysterograph is an instrument which predetermines how healthy a woman's childbirth will be.

Planned Parenthood begins a long-range education and research program leading the way in responsible family planning.

Doctors Approve Of Nursery Schools As An Opportunity To Expand A Child's Creative Motor Skills, Interact With Other Children And Experience An Authority Figure Other Than Parents.

At A Seminar Conducted By Dr. Benjamin M. Spock And Dr. Gustave F. Weinfeld It Is Disclosed Moderation In Indulging An Infant's Demands Is The Most Effective Approach In Achieving A Relaxed State For The Mom And Her Baby.

Dr. John C. Montgomery, Speaking Before The Annual Convention Of The American Psychiatric Association, Believes Spanking A Child Before It's Two Years Old Is Not Effective And In Fact Is Harmful As The Infant Cannot Understand Why It's Being Spanked. Although He Is Against Spanking, The Doctor Did Concede That For Older Children Sometimes A Spanking Is Better Than Nagging.

Thumb Suckers Are Destined To Suck Lollypops, Chew Gum, Bite Pencils Or Lips, Twirl Hair Or Chomp On Cigars.

A Father's Relationship With His Children Is Far More Important Than The Amount Of Material Possessions He Can Buy Them.

Stuttering Arises Out Of Approach-Avoidance — A Conflict To Proceed Along With A Desire To Retreat And Usually Begins Between The Ages Of Three And Five.

According To Research Conducted At New York's Mount Sinai Hospital Child Guidance Clinic Emotionally Disturbed Children Express Their Feelings About Their Parents Through Drawings.

WHAT A YEAR IT WAS!

1950

IT'S TIME FOR JOKING AROUND

Contrary To The Popular Notion That Comic Books Are A Negative Influence On Children Leading To All Kinds Of Anti-Social Behaviors, The National Association For Mental Health Takes A Positive Stand Stating Comic Books Are A Reading Aid, Can Draw Attention To The Child's Anxieties Through Dream Interpretation And Definitely Do Not Lead The Children Into A Life Of Crime.

TIPS ON TELEVIEWING FOR KIDS

Some Reassuring Advice To Parents Concerned With The Amount Of Time Junior Is Spending In Front Of The Television Is Given In **Today's Health** Which Recommends:

- TV Not Be Banned;
- Allow The Child To Participate In Program Selection;
- Encourage Cultural Programs;
- Don't Use As A Babysitter Or To Calm Children Down;
- It's A Novelty, The Excitement Is Sure To Wear Off.

TACKLING THE DRINKING PROBLEM
Clinics For The Treatment Of Alcoholics Are Established In 28 States.

To help treat the estimated 30,000 alcoholics in the "dry" state of Mississippi, a new facility is being completed with 201 beds.

Female alcoholics have less control over their drinking than their male counterparts and tend to be more emotionally immature, while men drink more consistently and show stronger preference for drinking than women states research published in the **American Journal Of Psychiatry**.

According to **Alcoholics Anonymous** some women develop drinking problems because they have too much time on their hands and try to match the drinking habits of their husbands.

A survey taken at the University of Rochester reveals that college girls who don't drink have more dates than their drinking counterparts.

Symptoms Of Alcoholism:

- Craving for a daily drink at the same time
- Starting the day with a drink
- Interfering with your family
- Inner trembling if you don't drink
- Physical problems
- Lack of ambition
- Frequent sleazy bars
- Increased confidence when you drink

PEACHES ANYONE?

Too much orange juice could have a damaging effect on the oral cavity according to Dr. Henry Hicks of Greenwich, Connecticut, who suggests that on a weekly basis no more than two or three oranges or one grapefruit be consumed.

EAT A SWEET — BRUSH YOUR TEETH

This is the conclusion reached from studies conducted at Yale University where it is discovered that tooth decay can be avoided if the sugar is brushed away immediately after eating your favorite sweet.

LET'S START TRIMMING OFF SOME OF THAT FAT

More than 28% of Americans are overweight.

A WEIGHTY ISSUE

Research conducted at Northwestern University Medical School indicates excess weight may be a contributing factor to bone and joint disorders.

WHEN THIS PROFESSOR SPEAKS, YOU SHOULD LISTEN

Professor T.K. Cureton of the University of Illinois School of Physical Education sets down suggestions for getting into shape and staying there:
Walk briskly at least two miles a day or swim one-half hour every other day.
Eat properly, avoiding large amounts of animal fats, starches and sugars.
Eat soybeans and green and yellow vegetables.

JUST DON'T EXHALE ON ME PLEASE

Latest studies reveal that garlic may serve as a relaxant for frayed nerves thereby aiding in digestion.

PASS THE FERNS PLEASE

In recent tests, tablets containing chlorophyll eliminate body and breath odor from 90% of the fifty people tested.

A high-protein diet is found to strengthen the immune system according to an article published in the "Journal Of Infectious Diseases."

Before he finally winds up on your Thanksgiving table, the turkey attempts suicide many times through a series of mishaps ranging from making friends with turkey-eating beasts, high blood pressure growing out of fear of surroundings, not eating properly or getting stuck in crevices.

High cholesterol diets are linked to arteriosclerosis.

Patients placed on a low fat and low cholesterol diet show marked reduction in the number of cholesterol-bearing defective molecules thought to contribute to hardening of the arteries.

BUT, IN THE MEANTIME PASS THE DREYER'S

Faced with the lack of calcium in the diet of most Americans, the State University of Iowa College of Medicine publishes a paper in "The Journal Of The American Medical Association " recommending adults drink a pint of milk daily and eat at least one serving of a milk product such as cheese or ice cream.

A Philadelphia cardiologist reports that it is dangerous for a heart patient to become completely inactive and that moderate work and activity is far less damaging than doing nothing.

Nothing like it on the road!

The new front appearance will delight you! So simple, so balanced, so graceful!

Sweeping new look to set the style pace!

New 1951 MERCURY with MERC-O-MATIC Drive

YOUR first *look* will tell you that the 1951 Mercury is a car brimming over with eye-filling features: new styling, new interiors, new trim.

Your first *drive* will tell you that here is an automobile with everything: honeyed smoothness, family comfort, safety, and economy.

And the 1951 Mercury offers you Merc-O-Matic—the smoother, simpler, more efficient automatic transmission developed and built exclusively for Ford Motor Company by Ford and Borg-Warner engineers.

In fact, with Mercury for 1951 you have a *triple* choice for "the drive of your life"—new Merc-O-Matic Drive and thrifty Touch-O-Matic Overdrive are optional at extra cost, and in addition there's the silent-ease synchronized standard transmission.

Get the complete story today from your Mercury dealer.

MERCURY DIVISION • FORD MOTOR COMPANY

New rear window—over 1000 square inches for safer visibility!

90

ONE, TWO, THREE, CHA CHA CHA

A patent is issued to Leo R. Smith for his tiny vibrator to be used on Christmas trees which causes the tinsel and glittering balls to move slightly, creating a dance and sparkle effect.

Europe gets its first SELF-SERVICE LAUNDRY

thanks to two American businessmen who install laundry machines in Vienna.

PRODUCTS OF TOMORROW

- Fish flown in fresh from the tropics for local markets
- Complete meals prepared and then frozen
- Edible bottles and cans
- A dipping chemical that will clean and dry dishes
- A foil for cooking meat which will evaporate when cooking is completed
- A laundry compound that will wash and dry clothes

WHAT A YEAR IT WAS!

1950

Still ticking after all these "accidents"

The "Almost Indestructible" low-priced **TIMEX** watch is introduced by the U.S. Time Corp.

Tell Him I'll Be There As Soon As I Put On My Lipstick

A combination telephone and television set is developed by the Army Signal Corps.

There Goes The Old "My Alarm Didn't Go Off" Excuse

General Electric introduces "The Repeater," an alarm clock that automatically resets itself to ring at the same time every 24 hours.

Bicycle riders can feel safer now that *Westinghouse* has created a bicycle lamp which can be seen a block away.

TAPE NOW, PLAY LATER

In development is a new radio-television unit equipped with a built-in tape recorder for recording radio shows.

A new folding snack table hits the market for use when watching television.

GENERAL ELECTRIC

introduces two new white fluorescent lights.

A RECORD AT ANY SPEED

A new record player in Zenith radio and television console combinations is capable of playing records of any speeds without changing needles.

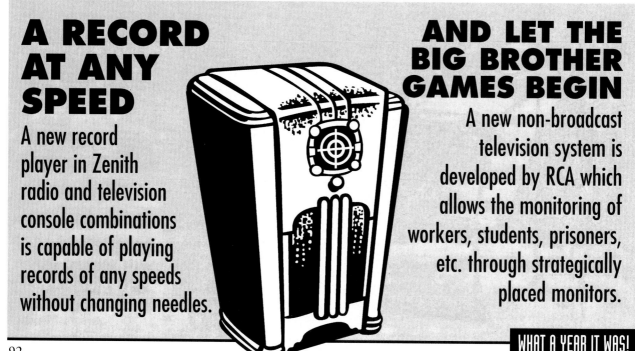

AND LET THE BIG BROTHER GAMES BEGIN

A new non-broadcast television system is developed by RCA which allows the monitoring of workers, students, prisoners, etc. through strategically placed monitors.

WHAT A YEAR IT WAS!

a face in the mirror

Non-fogging mirrors for bathroom cabinets are introduced by the Charles Parker Company, Meriden, Connecticut.

Oh thank goodness, I was worried for a moment
In case of an atomic attack you can now wear atom-resistant eyeglasses to protect you from the effects of that nasty fall-out.

The American Optical Company
develops eyeglasses using shatter-proof glass similar to that used on car windshields.

You can now light up a cigarette while driving thanks to a new automatic automobile cigarette lighter developed by Dowi Products in Milwaukee.

Cadillac introduces a one-piece curved windshield continuing to earn its reputation as the best in American luxury cars.

GOODYEAR
Develops Puncture-Sealing Tires.

A new automatic fare box is introduced in Chicago for buses which collects the coins and dispenses the correct change.

PUT AWAY THOSE SHAVING CUPS & BRUSHES, BOYS

Men can now get their shaving cream from a pressurized can which holds enough cream to lather up for almost 60 shaves.

AN INSTANT COOLING DOWN

A tiny battery-operated fan that fits in the palm of your hand is introduced by Rodorn, Inc. in New York City.

COOLING OFF
THE HOT SEAT

Two Texas manufacturers introduce a cooling unit for automobiles which can cool off a car's interior from 100° to 70° in just a few minutes.

WHAT A YEAR IT WAS!

1950

MINNESOTA MINING AND MANUFACTURING

develops a machine that enables mass production of sound tapes.

SONY MARKETS ITS FIRST TAPE RECORDER IN JAPAN.

AND NO COFFEE BREAKS EITHER

200 employees may soon be replaced by 20 machines that process orders for mail-order companies.

IT SURE BEATS THE PONY EXPRESS

Messages now move quicker than ever with the development of a nationwide system of high-speed telegraph message centers.

General Electric *develops a robot for use in handling radioactive materials.*

Hi, my name is Dave and I'll be handling your titanium.

Neither rain nor hail

Able to function under the most severe weather conditions, the Western Union Telegraph Company develops the world's first radio beam transmission system.

Washington DC gets its first desk-fax machines along with nine other U.S. cities.

The first radio paging service is launched in New York.

NO MORE FUMBLING FOR THE CORD

An automatic parachute is developed at the Wright-Patterson Air Force Base containing a sensor that causes the parachute to open at an elevation of 5,000 feet above the ground.

WHAT A YEAR IT WAS!

■ IBM ■

develops an artificial arm operated by one's toes, allowing amputees to answer telephones, write, light cigarettes and unlock doors.

A surgery patient can now administer his own anesthesia automatically thanks to a new machine called "Servo-Anesthetizer" developed by Dr. Reginald G. Bickford, Director of the Electro-Encephalography Laboratory of the Mayo Foundation.

A new hospital bed is developed with push-button controls allowing the patient to adjust the bed to different angles and is also equipped with a food tray, washbasin and exercise bar.

Well, if that ain't the cat's meow

Now you can go away for those long weekends and not worry about your pet dying of hunger as a new automatic feeding device is introduced which holds up to a week's supply of food and water.

No Cats allowed

PERMANENT PLASTIC HEADRESTS FOR USE ON PLANES, TRAINS AND BUSES IS DEVELOPED IN PASSAIC, NEW JERSEY BY THE HOWARD ZINK CORP.

A **HEARING AID WITH THE EAR PIECE ABOUT THE SIZE OF A SHIRT BUTTON HITS THE MARKET.**

A dishwashing device with a handle designed to hold liquid detergent which is dispensed automatically by pushing a button is released by the 20th Century Machine Co. of Hazel Park, Michigan.

An antiseptic liquid creamy hand soap is developed for hospitals and food and industrial workers.

SOAP

1950

A new coffee percolator that whistles when perking commences is being marketed by Perc-Tone Aluminum Products of Brooklyn, New York.

SLICING YOUR BUTTER AND SERVING IT TOO

A combination butter server and slicer is developed by Paul Industries located in New York City.

Skin and rind of citrus fruits can now be easily removed with a new plastic peeler introduced by The Dale Sales Corp. in New York.

NO MORE COLD MASHED POTATOES

A table-top warming device designed to keep food warm is invented by the Appleman Art Glass Company in Bergenfield, New Jersey.

GENERAL ELECTRIC introduces the first refrigerator with self-sealing magnetic doors.

Nothing Like A Bowl Of Sugar For Breakfast

Kids get to eat a new cereal called Sugar Pops.

Concentrated milk and Minute Rice hit the consumer market.

And Speaking Of Making Life Sweeter

Britain's Abbott Labs answer the diabetics craving for sugar with its non-sugar sweetener sucaryl sodium.

A home popcorn popping machine is developed in Memphis, Tennessee.

THERE'S MAD MONEY IN THEM THERE THIGHS

Ladies can safely hide their money in a new money belt shaped like a garter which is worn discreetly on their thigh.

The first copying machine to use xerography is introduced by the Haloid Company of Rochester, N.Y.

A machine that can collate 25,000 sheets an hour is being distributed by the Harris-Seybold Co. of Cleveland, Ohio.

188 banks in 54 cities can now speed up the transfer of money through the use of the newly introduced bank wire.

New York's Arnold Neustadter revolutionizes the way we store names and addresses with his rolodex address system.

The Royal Typewriter Company

announces the development of a new electrically controlled touch typewriter which allows easy transition from manual to electric.

Is That A Nickel I See In That Roll?

Banks no longer have to count coins out one at a time now that there's a new coin-packaging machine which counts, packages and boxes 1,000 coins a minute.

SHOOT & SHIP

A pre-loaded camera packed with a mailing carton saves you trips to your local drugstore as after you shoot the roll of film, you mail the camera back to the Photo-Pac Camera Mfg. Co., in Dallas, Texas and they will return your developed prints and negatives by mail.

WHAT A YEAR IT WAS!

ARCHITECTURE

The **Frank Lloyd Wright** designed V.C. Morris Shop attracts attention on San Francisco's Maiden Lane, where curious onlookers force the street's temporary closure to autos. Across the country, architecture's grand old man causes controversy by insulting a current courthouse project in a small Wisconsin town and offering his services for half-price. Also in Wisconsin, his lab for Johnson Wax opens.

Prevalent home styles include the Ranch and Cape Cod.

Nearly 24 million Americans are homeowners, while construction of new units reaches an all-time high — almost 1,400,000 units.

A model is shown of Ludwig Mies van der Rohe's latest creation — glass and steel apartments for Chicago's Lake Shore Drive.

WHAT A YEAR IT WAS!

Two massive housing projects are under way in California–Los Angeles' Park La Brea and San Francisco's Parkmerced. When finished, over 7,500 new apartments will be available.

Students occupy the Walter Gropius designed Commons Building at Harvard.

Men might not make passes at girls who wear glasses, but they're sure to notice girls who live in glass houses. A wall of windows brings the outside in and opens up your living space.

P.T. Barnum's old estate on Long Island will be developed into 400 homes, priced from just over $10,000.

UCLA's $15 Million Medical Center Is Under Construction.

Worried About Not Blending In With The Crowd?

A camouflage house, on view at a New York home furnishings show, makes it virtually impossible for enemy pilots to land a bomb on your doorstep.

WHAT A YEAR IT WAS!

1950

CHARLES EAMES

doesn't rest on his laurels, but continues to improve his modern chair design using Zenaloy (plastic with fiberglass) in the new, sleek models. His latest compact and colorful storage units work equally well in any room of the house.

*i*nnovative mixed material furniture – such as wood and metal tables – gain in popularity.

French fashion king *Jacques Fath* is now designing fashionable carpets for the home.

The question of what to wear to bed is only matched by what your bed should wear. This year's answer is plaid, in any light color, made of cotton, wool and/or rayon.

The first "Good Design" exhibit and competition cosponsored by Chicago's Merchandise Mart and New York's Museum of Modern Art features hundreds of interior designs including flatware, lamps, coffee tables, Baccarat glass, Eero Saarinen chairs, a Charles Eames table and a Georg Jensen jug.

BLACK CHINA *is now for sale at* MACY'S

Parchment, Sandalwood, Terra Cotta, Avocado, Navy, Citron, Pewter **KOOL COLORS FOR WALLS, FLOORS AND FURNITURE** Heather, Willow, Flame, Hyacinth

The exquisitely decorated living rooms of Elizabeth Arden & Mrs. Danny Kaye are voted two of the nicest in New York City.

WHAT A YEAR IT WAS!

Donald O'Connor and other Hollywood stars say good-bye as they leave to entertain our troops in Germany.

10 Box Office Draws

Bud Abbott & Lou Costello
Bing Crosby
Betty Grable
Bob Hope
Randolph Scott
James Stewart
Spencer Tracy
John Wayne
Clifton Webb
Esther Williams

John Wayne

Betty Grable

Bob Hope

New Kids in Tinseltown

Arlene Dahl
Joanne Dru
William Holden
Dean Jagger
John Lund
William Lundigan
Dean Martin & Jerry Lewis
Ruth Roman
Vera-Ellen
James Whitmore

"Samson And Delilah" is Top Earner Of The Year

Hi Ho, Hi Ho, It's Off To Sanwa Bank We Go

Box office records are set in Japan as Walt Disney's *SNOW WHITE* hits Japanese movie houses.

What?? No Mickey Or Goofy Or Even Donald Duck!!

Disney's *TREASURE ISLAND* is its first movie without animation.

Golden Globe World Film Favorites

Jane Wyman & Gregory Peck

Sam Goldwyn predicts that television will cut Hollywood movie production by 70% questioning why people would "go out to see bad films when they can stay home" and watch bad television for nothing.

It is estimated that movie attendance has reached the lowest number since the Depression—3,000 movie theatres close nationwide.

It's Off To The Big Apple We Go

United Artists announces it's moving to New York and closing its Hollywood offices.

Charlie Chaplin kisses Mary Pickford for the first time as they sell their jointly-owned 7,200 shares of United Artists stock for an estimated $4,000,000.

HOW ABOUT A MOVIE AND SOME NECKING?

Over 7,000,000 tickets a week sold at drive-in movies nationwide.

FAMOUS BIRTHS

Tom Berenger
Ed Harris
William Hurt
John Landis
William H. Macy
Amy Madigan
Leonard Maltin
Melissa Mathison
Bill Murray
Randy Quaid
John Sayles
Martin Short
Michael Tolkin
Jerry Zucker

WHAT A YEAR IT WAS!

The Academy Awards For 1950

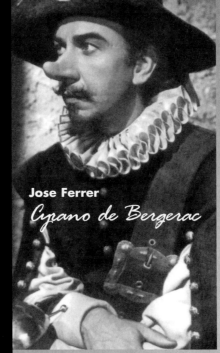

Jose Ferrer
Cyrano de Bergerac

"And The Winner Is..."

BEST PICTURE
All About Eve

BEST ACTOR
JOSE FERRER,
Cyrano de Bergerac

BEST ACTRESS
JUDY HOLLIDAY,
Born Yesterday

BEST DIRECTOR
JOSEPH L.
MANKIEWICZ,
All About Eve

BEST SUPPORTING ACTOR
GEORGE SANDERS, *All About Eve*

BEST SUPPORTING ACTRESS
JOSEPHINE
HULL, *Harvey*

BEST SONG
"MONA LISA,"
*Captain Carey,
U.S.A.*

Gary Merrill, Celeste Holm
and Bette Davis
All About Eve

1950

1950

All About Eve

American Guerrilla In The Philippines

Annie Get Your Gun

Armored Car Robbery

The Asphalt Jungle

The Big Hangover

THE BIG LIFT

The Black Rose

Born Yesterday

Broken Arrow

CAGED

Captain Carey, U.S.A.

Chain Lightning

Cheaper By The Dozen

Cinderella

CRISIS

Cyrano de Bergerac

D.O.A.

DANCE HALL

DARK CITY

The Daughter of Rosie O'Grady

DESTINATION MOON

Destination Murder

FANCY PANTS

Father Is A Bachelor

Father Of The Bride

Flesh & Blood

Fortunes Of Captain Blood

THE FURIES

The Glass Menagerie

Grandma Moses

THE GUNFIGHTER

THE HAPPIEST DAYS OF YOUR LIFE

HARVEY

IN A LONELY PLACE

The Jackie Robinson Story

Key To The City
King Solomon's Mines
Kiss Tomorrow Goodbye
La Beaute du Diable
La Ronde
The Lawless
Let's Dance
Magnificent Yankee
THE MEN
My Blue Heaven
My Friend Irma Goes West
THE NEXT VOICE YOU HEAR
Night And The City
No Man Of Her Own
No Sad Songs For Me
NO WAY OUT
ORPHEE
THE OUTRIDERS
PAID IN FULL
Panic In The Streets
Perfect Strangers
RASHOMON
Riding High
RIO GRANDE

ROCKETSHIP X-M
Rogues Of Sherwood Forest
The Secret Fury
SIDE STREET
The Sleeping City
Stage Fright
STATE SECRET
Stromboli
Summer Stock
THE SUNDOWNERS
SUNSET BOULEVARD
Tea For Two
THREE CAME HOME
Three Little Words
To Please A Lady
The Toast Of New Orleans
TREASURE ISLAND
Under My Skin
UNION STATION
Wagonmaster
Walk Softly, Stranger
WHERE THE SIDEWALK ENDS
The White Tower
Winchester '73
The Winslow Boy
Young Man With A Horn

Celebs Turn Out For
Noel Coward Picture

New York's swank Park Avenue Theatre lights up for an opening that is one of the top events of the season.

NOEL COWARD attends the premiere of his latest masterpiece—*The Astonished Heart*—with his long-time friend, **REX HARRISON.**

Society's **ELSA MAXWELL** *(left)* adds to the festivities.

Radio's ALLEN PRESCOTT interviews Noel Coward and Rex Harrison and the man who's created so many screen masterpieces does it again in this Universal International feature.

BURGESS MEREDITH and **JOYCE CAREY,** who is in the cast, also attend this gala event.

The premiere receipts are being donated to the Mary MacArthur fund to help victims of infantile paralysis.

WHAT A YEAR IT WAS!

Rep. King Asks For Repeal Of Movie Tax

In between the coming attractions, cartoon, newsreel and movie, Rep. King makes an appeal to the movie audience to sign up in the lobby to support repeal of the 20% federal tax they pay on their ticket.

William Holden

refuses to appear in a new picture called *Remember My Face* and is promptly suspended by **Columbia Studios.**

Major Film Stars Now Allowed To Appear On **Television** As Hollywood Studios Lift The Ban On Such Appearances.

Include Me In!

A lawsuit charging 20th Century Fox with trying to monopolize film distribution is filed by Fox competitor **Samuel Goldwyn** to the tune of $6,750,000.

Two For The Price Of One

Radio-Keith-Orpheum Corporation forms two separate parent companies — R.K.O. Pictures and R.K.O. Theatres and applies to list their common stock on the New York Stock Exchange.

Don't Get Mad— Get Even

Miffed at Columbia Pictures boss **Harry Cohn**, **Garson Kanin** demands and gets one million dollars for screen rights to *Born Yesterday*—the highest amount ever paid for a property.

A Tragic Day For The Hollywood Blacklist

Compiling names from the Justice Department's subversive list and other sources, anti-Communist American business consultants publish "Red Channels: The Report of Communist Influence in Radio and Television" in which entertainers **Lee J. Cobb, Lee Grant, Pete Seeger, Zero Mostel** and **Orson Welles** and 146 other "suspected entertainers" are named without any verification as to the truth. The publishers refuse to remove anyone's name unless that person joins or works for a pro-American organization or makes a full public confession before the House Un-American Activities Committee.

I Refuse To Answer On The Grounds That It Is Un-American

Fearing government censorship of motion pictures, the National Council of Arts, Sciences and Professionals sends a delegation to Washington to petition President Truman and the U.S. Supreme Court to set aside contempt of Congress rulings against ten Hollywood writers resulting from their refusal to disclose if they are Communists to the House Un-American Activities Committee.

Convictions of "Hollywood Ten" screenwriters upheld by the Supreme Court.

CROSLEY *Family Theatre Television*

gives you
FULL ROOM VISION

...with the new wide-angle Family Theatre Screen

Clear Big Pictures — Full Room Vision on this Crosley Family Theatre Screen

ORDINARY VIEWING | CROSLEY VIEWING

17 INCH Console Model 11-460 (Rectangular Tube). Stunning cabinet with bow front, rich mahogany veneer.

17 INCH Console Model 11-483 (Rectangular Tube). Blond wood veneers make a gorgeous cabinet.

17 INCH Table Model 11-442 (Rectangular Tube). Compactly beautiful in a mahogany veneer cabinet.

19 INCH Console Model 11-484 (Round Tube). Cabinet superbly finished in blond wood veneer.

17 INCH Console Model 11-470 (Rectangular Tube). Handsome cabinet of blond wood veneer.

THE PACE-SETTING DESIGNS ARE COMING FROM CROSLEY!

PASSINGS

Showman **Sid Grauman**, pioneer of large and ornate movie theatres and mastermind of the grand, flashy movie premiere, dies at age 70. Hollywood's Grauman's Chinese Theatre, where movie stars immortalize their hands, feet and other body parts, is known by film fans throughout the world.

Former vaudevillian **Walter Huston**, whose son John directed him in an Academy Award winning role in *The Treasure Of The Sierra Madre*, dies the day after his 66th birthday in Beverly Hills.

Best remembered for starring in *The Jazz Singer*, his performances in blackface, being the first entertainer to play for troops in World War II and his classic saying *"You ain't heard nothing yet,"* **Al Jolson**, son of a rabbi/cantor, dies at age 66.

THE THREE SEXIEST MEN & WOMEN IN THE WORLD
(Chosen By Hollywood Women Extras)

Montgomery Clift   Ava Gardner
Howard Duff   Lana Turner
Tyrone Power   Jane Russell

HOLLYWOOD'S ALL-TIME GREATEST LOVERS

John Barrymore	*Theatrical flair for love*
Charles Boyer	*Suave lover*
Clark Gable	*Beat-me-up anytime lover*
John Gilbert	*Dashing lover*
Rudolph Valentino	*The Latin lover*

The Best Of The First 50 Years
(A Variety Poll)

Best Director: **D.W. Griffith**
Best Producer: **Irving Thalberg**
Best Actor: **Charlie Chaplin**
Best Actress: **Greta Garbo**
Best Film: **"Gone With The Wind"**

I'm Ready For My Award Mr. DeMille

Billy Wilder *(left)*, Gloria Swanson and Erich von Stroheim on *Sunset Boulevard* set.

The 25th annual poll conducted by the National Board of Review of Motion Pictures chooses **Billy Wilder's** SUNSET BOULEVARD, with its riveting performance by **Gloria Swanson**, as the Best American Film Of The Year followed by ALL ABOUT EVE, THE ASPHALT JUNGLE, THE MEN, EDGE OF DOOM, TWELVE O'CLOCK HIGH, PANIC IN THE STREETS, CYRANO DE BERGERAC, NO WAY OUT and STAGE FRIGHT.

All About Luck And Timing

Although both actresses receive the highest critical acclaim for their stunning performances in SUNSET BOULEVARD and ALL ABOUT EVE, Gloria Swanson and **Bette Davis** were not actually first casting choices and it was only after **Mae West, Mary Pickford** and **Pola Negri** turned down the role of the aging actress in SUNSET BOULEVARD and **Claudette Colbert** cracked a rib knocking her out of ALL ABOUT EVE did Swanson and Davis land the roles.

Take This You Dirty Pro-Censorship Dog

No definitive connection can be found between juvenile delinquency and movies according to sociologists and psychiatrists enlisted by the Council of Motion Picture Organizations. Their opinion is shared by George Stoddard, president of the University of Illinois, who feels that the behavior problems lie not with films "but with the quality of home and neighborhood life."

1950

Unknown actor **LLOYD BRIDGES** slotted to star in Civil War classic **The Red Badge Of Courage**.

GOING OUT WITH A COMMERCIAL WHIMPER

Atoll K is **Laurel & Hardy's** last film together and unfortunately scores very little success.

No Longer Skating On Thin Ice

Champion skater and Hollywood actress **SONJA HENIE** becomes U.S. citizen.

SIDNEY POITIER makes his cinematic debut in **No Way Out**.

HEY ABBOTT!

Funnymen **Bud Abbott** and **Lou Costello** celebrate their 15th year together vowing to stay together for 15 more.

No Fiddling Around On This One

Convinced that *QUO VADIS*, the epic drama about Nero's Rome, is going to be a hit, M-G-M's **Louis B. Mayer** coughs up a $6,000,000 production budget, the biggest in movie history, and sends a crew to Italy for pre-production work.

While at the wedding reception celebrating his marriage to Patrice Wymore, **Errol Flynn** is served with a summons concerning his alleged rape of a 15-year old French girl on his yacht.

The Destruction Of A Beautiful Actress' Career

Ingrid Bergman, who fled America because of the attacking press and negative public sentiment over her extramarital affair with **Roberto Rossellini**, gives birth to his son in Rome.

AN EXPANDING ROLE

Glamorous movie stars **June Allyson**, **Jane Powell** and **Esther Williams** are all expecting babies.

Thurber Carnival is the title of a movie being developed based on the cartoons and short stories of **James Thurber** which will be a combination of live action and animation.

Hey Stella, Get The Ice

MARLON BRANDO is laid up for three days as a result of the reactivation of an old shoulder injury during the filming of A STREETCAR NAMED DESIRE.

Despite being omitted from the list of new young actors in Hollywood, **MARLON BRANDO** captures critical acclaim for his stunning performance in THE MEN in which he plays a World War II paraplegic.

GEE FELLAS NO BIKINI WATCHING THIS YEAR

Due to insufficient funding the Cannes Film Festival is cancelled.

RADIO

TOP DAYTIME AM RADIO SHOWS

GRAND CENTRAL STATION
ARMSTRONG THEATRE
CEDRIC ADAMS
STARS OVER HOLLYWOOD
ROMANCE OF HELEN TRENT
OUR GAL SUNDAY
WHEN A GIRL MARRIES
PORTIA FACES LIFE
MA PERKINS
WENDY WARREN
TRUE DETECTIVE MYSTERIES
THE SHADOW
ARTHUR GODFREY
MARTIN KANE
AUNT JENNY

LONG-RUNNING PROGRAMS
GO OFF THE RADIO DIAL

BLONDIE

BURNS and ALLEN

DR. I.Q.

The FRED WARING Show

JACK ARMSTRONG, The All-American Boy

TODAY'S CHILDREN

The TOM MIX Ralston Straightshooters

TOP EVENING AM RADIO SHOWS

RADIO THEATRE
JACK BENNY SHOW
MY FRIEND IRMA
CHARLIE McCARTHY
GODFREY'S TALENT SCOUTS
AMOS 'N' ANDY
CRIME PHOTOGRAPHER
YOU BET YOUR LIFE
LIFE WITH LUIGI
MYSTERY THEATRE
FIBBER McGEE & MOLLY
WALTER WINCHELL
INNER SANCTUM

1950

THAT KIND OF HAS A FAMILIAR RING TO IT

The famous NBC chimes used for the last 23 years become the first trademark granted by the U.S. Patent Office for a musical phrase.

DO YOU SOLEMNLY SWEAR TO NEVER PLOT TO GIVE AWAY THE PLOT?

CBS demands its employees including radio and television performers to sign a loyalty oath.

YOUR FRIENDLY NEIGHBORHOOD MONSTER

BORIS KARLOFF is hired by radio station WNEW in New York for a children's show where he will read poetry, play music and tell stories.

With her son Elliott as announcer, **ELEANOR ROOSEVELT** replaces Mary Margaret McBride on her daily WNBC radio program.

You Gotta Have Heart

In a charity event to benefit the Heart Fund, Speaker of the House **SAM RAYBURN** beats out fellow Washington politicians including Vice President and Mrs. Alben Barkley and is winning performer on **TED MACK'S ORIGINAL AMATEUR HOUR.**

He'll Get Lots Of Kicks From Champagne

FRANK SINATRA is ecstatic over his new three-year contract with CBS calling for 39 weeks at an annual salary of over $250,000.

He'd Rather Switch Than Fight

Two days after Lever Brothers drops **BOB HOPE** in the middle of his 10-year contract, the comedian announces a record-breaking new 5-year radio and television deal with NBC at a weekly salary of $30,000 for 39 weeks a year just for radio appearances.

What? And Give Up Show Business?

To celebrate the 200th anniversary of Bach's death, conductor of the Philadelphia Orchestra **LEOPOLD STOKOWSKI** becomes the lowest paid disc jockey in the country as he signs up to do a four-week show for WNBC at a pay scale of $1.00 for playing his own recordings of Bach compositions.

1950 ADVERTISEMENT

KEY SAFE
By Mail **89¢** *Postpaid*

Never again need you be locked out of your car or be without your ignition key. Insert a spare key in Key Safe's chamber, snap the box shut. Then conceal Key Safe on any metal part of your car—under bumper, frame, or fender. Husky magnet won't let go; key won't rattle. Key Safe costs only 89c. No. GM 3555.

Write for Big Catalog . . . Free

The Unusual

Miles Kimball
KIMBALL BUILDING
100 BOND ST., OSHKOSH, WIS.

WHAT A YEAR IT WAS!

This Victrola "45"—a complete automatic phonograph, not an attachment—takes up less than 1 cubic foot of space. Sounds better, plays "easier," costs less! RCA Victor 45EY. AC. **$29⁹⁵**

Victrola "45"

● This new System of recorded music has proved its popularity by its rocketing sales—65,000 automatic changers, a million and a half records a *month* . . . it's sweeping the country!

Over 2000 selections are now on 45 rpm records. The little, 7-inch, non-breakable discs can play as long as ordinary 10- and 12-inch, last up to 10 times longer.

"Here Come the Dance Bands Again"—Your favorite all-time hits are now on "45"—specially arranged for dancing. 15 great albums, each by a big name band!

Imagine a complete Victrola radio-phonograph with full-size tone—yet just 1½ feet wide, less than 2½ feet high! Has AM radio and the world's finest, simplest, *surest* automatic record changer, the RCA Victor "45." AC. RCA Victor 9W51. **$99⁹⁵**

Newest in recorded music . . .
Newest in radio too!

Tone you could never get before in a Table Radio

There's a giant, 8-inch console-size speaker in this dramatic little table radio. And it has the famous "Golden Throat"—finest tone system in RCA Victor history. Result—a depth, brilliance, range of tone you'd expect to get from a fine, full-size console! Has 3-point tone control. Cabinet is rich mahogany "Fine-Wood" finish on plastic, with a phono-jack for attaching a "45" record changer. AC. RCA Victor 9X571. **$39⁹⁵**

"Victrola"—T. M. Reg. U. S. Pat. Off.

The "45" automatic record changer attachment (not shown) which plugs right in to either of these radios, can easily be attached to *any* radio, phono or television set. It plays up to 10 of the new 45 rpm records automatically.
Only **$12⁹⁵**

This beauty in ultra-modern maroon plastic also has 8-inch console-size speaker and the "Golden Throat." A spectacular performer! RCA Victor 9X561. AC. **$29⁹⁵**

Tune in RCA Victor's "Screen Directors' Playhouse"—radio version of famous movies with the original movie star and director, Friday nights on the NBC radio network.

Prices shown are suggested list prices and are subject to change without notice. Slightly higher in far West and South.

RCA Victor
**WORLD LEADER IN RADIO
FIRST IN RECORDED MUSIC
FIRST IN TELEVISION**
DIVISION OF RADIO CORPORATION OF AMERICA

What's On Television This Week

Actors Studio
Al Morgan
The Alan Young Show
The Aldrich Family
American Forum Of The Air
Arthur Godfrey And His Friends
The Big Story
Big Top
Blind Date
Break The Bank
Broadway To Hollywood—Headline Clues
Can You Top This
Candid Camera
Cavalcade Of Bands
Cavalcade Of Stars
Celebrity Time
Chance Of A Lifetime
The Clock
The College Bowl
Don McNeill's TV Club
The Earl Wrightson Show
The Ed Sullivan Show
Famous Jury Trials
Fireside Theatre
Ford Star Revue
Ford Theatre
Four Star Revue
The Fred Waring Show
Garroway At Large
The Goldbergs
The Herb Shriner Show
Hopalong Cassidy

Kay Kyser's Kollege Of Musical Knowledge
Kraft Television Theatre
Kukla, Fran & Ollie
The Life Of Riley
Lights Out
The Lone Ranger
Lucky Pup
Magic Cottage
Mama

Man Against Crime
Martin Kane, Private Eye
Meet The Press
The Milton Berle Show
The Morey Amsterdam Show
On Trial
One Man's Family
Original Amateur Hour
Paul Whiteman's Goodyear Revue
Penthouse Party
The Perry Como Show
Philco TV Playhouse
The Plainclothesman
Presidential Timber
Pulitzer Prize Playhouse
Red Barber's Corner
Ripley's Believe It Or Not
Roller Derby
The Ruggles
Studio One
Studs' Place
This Is Show Business
Toast Of The Town
Tom Corbett, Space Cadet
Treasury Men In Action
Twenty Questions
Visit With The Armed Forces
The Voice Of Firestone
Wayne King
We The People
The Wendy Barrie Show
Who Said That

Kukla, Fran & Ollie

Paul Whiteman

Perry Como

114

WHAT A YEAR IT WAS!

And Premiering...

The Adventures Of Ellery Queen
Armstrong Circle Theatre
The Arthur Murray Party
Beat The Clock
Buck Rogers
The Cisco Kid
The Colgate Comedy Hour
Danger
Dick Tracy
The Frank Sinatra Show
The Garry Moore Show
The Gene Autry Show
The George Burns And Gracie Allen Show
Holiday Hotel
The Jack Benny Show
The Jack Carter Show
The Ken Murray Show
Life Begins At 80
Lux Video Theatre
The Marshall Of Gunsight Pass
Pantomime Quiz
The Peter Lind Hayes Show
Robert Montgomery Presents
Rocky King,
   Inside Detective
Showtime, U.S.A.
Somerset Maugham
   TV Theatre
Songs For Sale
Star Of The Family
The Steve Allen Show *(premieres on Christmas Day)*
The Stu Erwin Show
Truth Or Consequences
Van Camp's Little Show
The Vaughn Monroe Show
The Web
We Take Your Word
What's My Line
You Bet Your Life
Your Hit Parade
Your Show Of Shows

W. Somerset Maugham

Almost 5,000,000 Television Sets Are Now In Use Nationwide.

RCA chairman **David Sarnoff** announces that *"we are on the threshold of a new era in television—the era of color,"* as his company unveils its all-electronic color television tube.

Declaring CBS the best of all the color systems it had seen, the FCC authorizes CBS to begin broadcasting in color. Fearing CBS domination RCA goes to court in Chicago to block commencement of color broadcasting and wins temporary restraining order.

Television gets its first made-for-television movie as the Magnavox Corp. airs the Hal Roach Studio's $25,000 production of **THE THREE MUSKETEERS**.

FAMOUS BIRTHS

**Christine Lahti
Cybill Shepherd
David Cassidy
Jane Pauley
Jay Leno
Joan Lunden
Markie Post
Victoria Principal**

❑ The Nation's 100th Television Station Begins Operation In Ames, Iowa At Iowa State College, Becoming The First College-Owned Television Station.

❑ More And More New Yorkers Are Switching Off Their Radios And Turning On Their Television Sets.

❑ Baltimore Becomes First U.S. City Where More People Are Watching Television Than Listening To The Radio.

❑ National Sponsors Abandon Radio And Switch To Television In Record Numbers.

❑ California-Based Short Line Bus Company Thrills Its Passengers As It Installs The First Television Set On One Of Its Buses.

❑ Television Thought To Have A Good Future In The Military For Lectures And Observation Of Maneuvers.

EMMY awards

SERIES

DRAMATIC	**Pulitzer Prize Playhouse**
VARIETY	**The Alan Young Show**
CHILDREN'S	**Time For Beany**

PERFORMERS

ACTOR	**Alan Young**
ACTRESS	**Gertrude Berg**
PERSONALITY	**Groucho Marx**

Predicting that women will be a strong voice in television production within a few years, TV executives begin letting down some of the barriers to women entering the field.

Spurred by consumer complaints, New York City's Better Business Bureau sets up a code of selling and servicing practices for television.

NBC's The Saturday Night Revue, touted as the "biggest show in television," is also creating the biggest headaches, and with a $50,000 weekly cost it becomes the most expensive program ever developed.

Worried about the national **television craze** and present level of programming, Boston University president Dr. Daniel L. Marsh warns that "we are destined to be a **NATION OF MORONS**" if programming is not improved.

WHAT A YEAR IT WAS!

KING KONG WILL HAVE TO CLIMB A LITTLE HIGHER

EMPIRE STATE BUILDING managers agree to build a multiple antenna system after NBC agrees to give up its exclusive rights and share it with WJZ-TV, WABD and WPIX.

Jimmy Durante receives rave reviews for his new television show

Jimmy Durante wins a Peabody Award

Hitting A High Note In Her Career

Margaret Truman signs a contract with CBS for a weekly television show.

A Not So Chilling Experience

Bob Hope becomes first major radio comic to make the transition to television and receives a record salary of $40,000 for his appearance on a 90-minute variety show presented by Frigidaire on Easter night.

Read My Lips—We're Going Into Television

Charlie McCarthy's sidekick, ventriloquist **Edgar Bergen**, announces he's taking his show to television, signing up for three shows sponsored by Coca-Cola.

SAY THE MAGIC WORD AND WE SWITCH

Groucho Marx switches his *You Bet Your Life* program from CBS to NBC.

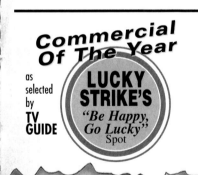

Commercial Of The Year

as selected by **TV GUIDE**

LUCKY STRIKE'S *"Be Happy, Go Lucky"* Spot

He's Back In The Saddle Again

America's first singing cowboy **Gene Autry** makes his television debut with sidekick Pat Buttram and ever-faithful horse, Champion.

GOD BLESS KATE SMITH

The Kate Smith Show is the first major daytime program to become successful.

Celebrities Seen And Heard On Television

Jack Lemmon	Robert Alda
Ralph Edwards	Dean Martin &
John Cameron	Jerry Lewis
Swayze	Dick Van Patten
Sid Caesar	Jackie Gleason
Imogene Coca	Art Carney
Carl Reiner	Bert Parks
Ralph Bellamy	Eva Marie Saint
Jan Murray	Mercedes
Rosemary Clooney	McCambridge
Tony Bennett	Tony Randall
Vincent Price	Eddie Cantor
Jackie Coogan	Fred Allen
Arlene Francis	Chico Marx
Martha Wright	Andy Williams
Don Ameche	Ed Wynn
Butterfly McQueen	Danny Thomas
Ethel Waters	Studs Terkel

Edie Adams Is Selected **Miss U.S. Television 1950**

Benny   *Burns & Allen*

Jack Benny

makes his TV debut using his radio format and old friends Eddie "Rochester" Anderson, Artie Auerbach, Don Wilson, The Sportsmen Quartet and special guest Dinah Shore. His other pals Phil Harris, Dennis Day and Mary Livingstone will be introduced on a later program.

Radio fans can now see their favorite zany

couple George Burns and Gracie Allen on television as the famous husband and wife team make the move to the tube.

"Is it bigger than a breadbox" becomes a national phrase as a result of the questions posed on television's *What's My Line*.

WHAT'S IN THAT LITTLE BLACK BOX

A.C. Nielson buys national television and radio Hooperatings and monitors 1,200 homes to sample television viewing habits.

Jerry Lester, alternating with **Morey Amsterdam**, hosts NBC's *Broadway Open House*, the first late-night television celebrity talk show.

ABC introduces children's Saturday morning programming with its *Animal Clinic* dealing with the care and maintenance of animals.

Laugh tracks for sitcoms is the only surviving legacy of *The Hank McCune Show*, the first television show to be cancelled mid-season.

MUSIC

1950 POPULAR SONGS

A Bushel And A Peck . . . . *Betty Hutton & Perry Como*

All I Want For Christmas Is My Two Front Teeth . . *Spike Jones*

All My Love (Bolero) . . . . *Patti Page*

Bewitched, Bothered & Bewildered . . . . *Bill Snyder & His Orchestra*

Bibbidi-Bobbidi-Boo . . . . *Perry Como*

C'est Si Bon . . . . *Johnny Desmond*

Choo'n Gum . . . . *Teresa Brewer*

The Cry Of The Wild Goose . . . . *Frankie Laine*

Dear Hearts And Gentle People . . . . *Bing Crosby*

Enjoy Yourself . . . . *Guy Lombardo & The Royal Canadians*

Goodnight Irene . . . . *The Weavers*

Harbor Lights . . . . *Sammy Kaye & His Orchestra*

Hoop-Dee-Doo . . . . *Perry Como with the Fontane Sisters*

I Can Dream, Can't I . . . . *The Andrews Sisters*

I Cross My Fingers . . . . *Perry Como*

I Wanna Be Loved . . . . *The Andrews Sisters*

If I Knew You Were Comin' I'd've Baked A Cake . . *Eileen Barton*

It Isn't Fair . . . . *Don Cornell*
                         with Sammy Kaye

La Vie en Rose . . . . *Edith Piaf*

Mona Lisa . . . . *Nat "King" Cole*

Mule Train . . . . *Frankie Laine*

My Foolish Heart . . . . *Billy Eckstine*

No Other Love . . . . *Jo Stafford*

The Old Master Painter . . . . *Richard Hayes*

On The Outgoing Tide . . . . *Perry Como*

Music! Music! Music! . . . . *Teresa Brewer*

Patricia . . . . *Perry Como*

Play A Simple Melody . . . . *Bing & Gary Crosby*

Rag Mop . . . . *The Ames Brothers*

Sentimental Me . . . . *The Ames Brothers*

Sisters . . . . *Rosemary & Betty Clooney*

Tennessee Waltz . . . . *Patti Page*

There's No Tomorrow . . . . *Tony Martin*

The Thing . . . . *Phil Harris*

Third Man Theme . . . . *Hugo Winterhalter*

Tzena, Tzena, Tzena . . . . *The Weavers*

White Christmas . . . . *Bing Crosby*

With My Eyes Wide Open I'm Dreaming . . . . *Patti Page*

You're Just In Love . . . . *Perry Como*

Nat "King" Cole

Bing Crosby

Doris Day

WHAT A YEAR IT WAS!

Brighten your Summer

WITH A COLOR STYLED

Portable

They're new, exciting, the smartest vacation radios yet. Sparkling G-E 3-way portables in a variety of gay colors to accent your own good taste and complement your favorite sportswear. Compact, sturdy, low-priced and light—most are only 8 lbs. with batteries. Take your choice of fawn tan, marine green, or maroon. Also a deluxe maroon model specially built to get distant stations. Whichever you choose you'll be sure of G-E excellence in power, tone, and dependability. Add "color" to your vacation with a new G-E portable. See them at your General Electric dealer's today.

General Electric Company, Electronics Park, Syracuse, N.Y.

Model 603, Fawn Tan
Model 601, Maroon
$29⁹⁵*

Model 604
Marine Green
$29⁹⁵*

Model 650
Warm Maroon
$39⁹⁵*

OTHER G-E PORTABLES
from **$19⁹⁵***

*Eastern prices, less batteries

You can put your confidence in —

GENERAL ⓖⒺ ELECTRIC

120

A COUNTRY MUSIC SAMPLER

A Bushel And A Peck . . . . *Jimmy Wakely*

Ain't Nobody's Business But My Own . . . . *Tennessee Ernie Ford*

Chattanoogie Shoe Shine Boy . . . . *Red Foley*

Daddy's Last Letter . . . . *Tex Ritter*

Don't Be Ashamed Of Your Age . . . . *Red Foley*

Frosty The Snow Man . . . . *Gene Autry*

I Love You Because . . . . *Ernest Tubb*

Ida Red Likes The Boogie . . . . *Bob Wills*

If You've Got The Money I've Got The Time . . *Lefty Frizzell*

Little Angel With The Dirty Face . . . . *Eddy Arnold*

Long Gone Lonesome Blues . . . . *Hank Williams*

My Son Calls Another Man Daddy . . . . *Hank Williams*

Peter Cottontail . . . . *Gene Autry*

Hank Williams

Bob Wills

Disc jockey
SAM PHILLIPS
forms the MEMPHIS
RECORDING SERVICE.

31-year old Hillbilly singer **TENNESSEE ERNIE FORD** goes from being an unknown to a popular star with his recording of THE CRY OF THE WILD GOOSE.

Folksinging group **THE WEAVERS** consisting of **LEE HAYS, PETE SEEGER, FRED HELLERMAN** and **RONNIE GILBERT**, whose careers were launched last year at Manhattan's VILLAGE VANGUARD, sell out TOWN HALL concerts and make appearances at the BLUE ANGEL nightclub.

The **UKULELE** is given professional status by the New York chapter of the American Federation of Musicians.

PETE SEEGER CREATES HOOTENANNY RECORD LABEL.

WHAT A YEAR IT WAS!

1950

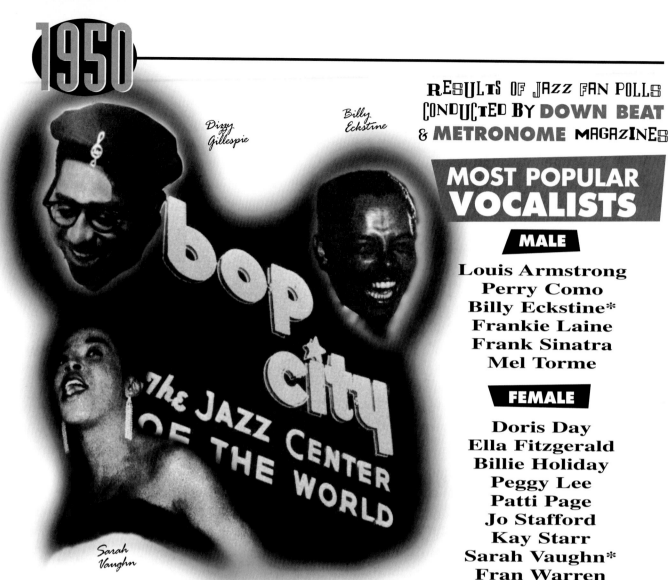

Dizzy Gillespie

Billy Eckstine

Sarah Vaughn

Disgusted With Having To Play "Ticky-Ticky-Tick" Dance Music DIZZY GILLESPIE Calls It Quits And Breaks Up His Band.

Jazz Great **Duke Ellington** And His 17-Man Band Play To A Wildly Enthusiastic Sell-Out Audience In **Amsterdam.**

THE MAMBO, a popular dance that came to New York via Cuba, begins catching on across the country and enthusiasts can move to the beat at New York's Palladium Ballroom or at the swanky Waldorf-Astoria.

- *Goodnight, Irene*, Written By Blues Legend **Huddie Ledbetter (Leadbelly)**, And Adapted By John Lomax, Holds No. 1 Position On The Charts For 13 Weeks.

- **Frank Sinatra** Suffers A Throat Hemorrhage During Nightclub Engagement In New York.

- Hollywood Film Star **Tallulah Bankhead** Makes Her First Singing Album.

Cool Jazz develops from bebop

WHAT A YEAR IT WAS!

1950

New Recording Artists

Teresa Brewer

Eddie Fisher

Mitch Miller & His Orchestra

Guy Mitchell

Les Paul & Mary Ford

19-Year Old Teresa Brewer Gets Her First Million-Seller Record With Her Recording Of Music, Music, Music.

FAMOUS BIRTHS

Bernie Taupin
Bobby McFerrin
Huey Lewis
Natalie Cole
Peter Frampton
Peter Gabriel
Teddy Pendergrass
Tom Petty

STEVIE WONDER

Bobby-Soxers Gather At New York's Paramount Theater To Cheer On Their New Heartthrob **Eddie Fisher** Whose Career Is Taking Off After Headlining At The Riviera Club.

King of **CORN**: Spike Jones
Runner-up: Guy Lombardo

- RCA Releases Its First LP Records.

- **Margaret Truman** Signs A Recording Contract With RCA Victor Red Seal Records.

- **Judy Garland, Ginger Rogers, Robert Montgomery, Faye Emerson, Dan Dailey** And **Sonja Henie** Among Show Biz Personalities Attending Opening Night Of **Edith Piaf's** Performance At New York's Versailles.

- South Pacific Star **Mary Martin** And Her 10-Year Old Son **Larry Hagman** Cut Their First Record Together.

Passings

One of the founders of Harlem's renowned Savoy Ballroom, **Sigmund Gale** passes on at age 77.

Co-founder of ASCAP, **Jay Witmark**, prominent music publisher whose successes include *Sweet Adeline* and *My Wild Irish Rose*, dies at age 77.

Kurt Weill, who began composing at age 12 and whose compositions have been performed in opera houses worldwide (*The Threepenny Opera*) as well as motion pictures (*Knickerbocker Holiday*), dies at age 50.

WHAT A YEAR IT WAS!

ARVIN announces....

First low-priced TV with these BIG SET features!

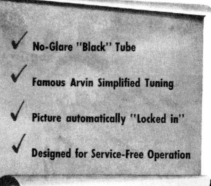

✓ No-Glare "Black" Tube

✓ Famous Arvin Simplified Tuning

✓ Picture automatically "Locked in"

✓ Designed for Service-Free Operation

ARVIN Visible Value TELEVISION

You can SEE the difference!

$129⁵⁰*

Plus Federal Tax—$1.26

Wide Angle Screen . . . Ideal for Apartments . . . as a "Second" Set!

You'll say it looks, tunes, and sounds like an expensive TV! That's because this amazing *Arvin Model Forty-Eighty is built like an expensive TV!*

Full 8½" No-Glare "Black" Tube insures clear, contrasty pictures. Only two visible groups of controls—easy as tuning a radio. Trouble-free electromagnetic circuit—straight AC operation for longer tube life and greater dependability. Horizontal automatic frequency control keeps picture locked in, even with high interference levels. Ask your Arvin Dealer to show you these and other important value features of the new Arvin Forty-Eighty. SEE IT AND HEAR IT—Now—at your dealer.

Arvin Radio and Television Division, Noblitt-Sparks Industries, Inc., Columbus, Indiana

*Price slightly higher in Zone 2

Model 3121 TM   Model 3120 CM   Model 3160 CM

ARVIN DELUXE LINE—TOP BIG-SCREEN VALUES

All deluxe models include built-in Versi-tenna and phono-jack.

Arvin Table Model 3121 TM, Giant 12½" Direct View Screen, includes all Arvin deluxe TV features: simplified tuning, Magic Moderator, surplus power for fringe areas. Mahogany finish; table to match at slight extra cost.

Arvin Console Model 3120 CM, Giant 12½" Direct View Screen at convenient eye level. Big-screen TV at small screen prices. All famous Arvin deluxe features. Mahogany finish.

Arvin Console Model 3160 CM—Super-oversize 16" Direct View Screen with clearer, steadier pictures actually measuring 14⅜ by 11¼ inches. Beautifully styled in genuine mahogany.

ON BROADWAY

Ethel Merman's CALL ME MADAM Racks Up The Biggest Advance Sales In Theatrical History To The Tune Of Over $1,000,000 With The Waiting List For Tickets Almost A Year Long.

Ethel Merman and Paul Lukas in *Call Me Madam.*

Julie Harris
in
*The Member
Of The
Wedding*

Pulitzer Prize for Drama

Richard Rodgers, Oscar Hammerstein II and Joshua Logan

SOUTH PACIFIC

The New York Drama Critics' Circle Awards

— BEST AMERICAN PLAY —
THE MEMBER OF THE WEDDING

— BEST FOREIGN PLAY —
THE COCKTAIL PARTY

— BEST MUSICAL —
THE CONSUL

WHAT A YEAR IT WAS!

★ **Uta Hagen** is cast in the lead role in the revival of the Pulitzer Prize winning play *A Streetcar Named Desire*.

★ **Paul Kelly** and **Uta Hagen** give sterling performances in **Clifford Odets'** *The Country Girl*, the story of life backstage and the career of an alcoholic actor.

★ *Hilda Crane* by **Samson Raphaelson** is the story of a career woman whose life ends in suicide.

★ **Boris Karloff** stars as Captain Hook in a revival of *Peter Pan*.

★ The average member of Actors Equity worked ten weeks as of June 1st earning $840 with one-quarter of the membership earning less than $335 in the same time period.

George Bernard Shaw

FAMOUS BIRTH
Wendy Wasserstein

PASSINGS

Shortly after whispering *"I want to sleep,"* 94-year old **George Bernard Shaw**, the most important playwright of his time, slips into a coma and never wakes up. In addition to his countless plays, including **Pygmalion** and **Man And Superman**, the Irishman is also known for his inimitable wit, strong belief in vegetarianism, Socialist leanings and winning the 1925 Nobel Prize for Literature.

Singer and actress **TESS GARDELLA**, lovingly known as Aunt Jemima, loses her battle with diabetes at age 52.

WHAT A YEAR IT WAS!

With his first play in eight years about to open on Broadway, playwright **William Saroyan** issues a warning that *The Son* is a depressingly bad play and advises everyone against seeing it.

He's Washing Broadway Right Out Of His Hair

In a sad farewell after signing a $1,000,000 Hollywood contract, *South Pacific* star **Ezio Pinza** leaves the cast of the award-winning Broadway play to pursue a film career.

It Must Have Been Something She Et

Mae West collapses onstage during a performance of *Diamond Lil* from what appears to be food poisoning.

Here Comes A Hit

Carson McCullers stage adaptation of her novel *The Member Of The Wedding* opens in New York at the Empire Theatre and wins Best Play of the Year award.

A Whole Bunch Of Chatter

T.S. Eliot's *The Cocktail Party* fares better in New York than in London.

Oh Senator—Whatever Do You Mean

Louis Verneuil's *Affairs Of State* is the story of love affairs in Washington DC.

Tony Awards 1950

OUTSTANDING PLAY
"The Cocktail Party"
T.S. Eliot (playwright)

OUTSTANDING MUSICAL
"South Pacific"

OUTSTANDING DRAMATIC ACTOR
Sidney Blackmer
"Come Back, Little Sheba"

OUTSTANDING DRAMATIC ACTRESS
Shirley Booth
"Come Back, Little Sheba"

OUTSTANDING MUSICAL ACTOR
Ezio Pinza
"South Pacific"

OUTSTANDING MUSICAL ACTRESS
Mary Martin
"South Pacific"

OUTSTANDING DIRECTOR
Joshua Logan
"South Pacific"

Alone And Awake He Looks At The Keys

Richard Rodgers hard at work on his new musical *Anna And The King Of Siam*.

Another Night, Another Opening, And It's Probably Theirs

Lee and Jacob Shubert, who own more than half of the nation's major legitimate theatres, are slapped with a civil antitrust suit by the Justice Department and are asked to sell enough of their theatres to restore competition.

AND ON THE OTHER SIDE OF THE OCEAN...

Tyrone Power

Following in the stage tradition of his grandfather and father, Hollywood's **Tyrone Power** is excited about his first performance on the London stage in a production of *Mr. Roberts*.

After 11 years of being dark, Britain reopens its Old Vic Theatre on Waterloo Road with a production of *Twelfth Night* performed by the Old Vic Company.

John Gielgud takes over as head of Stratford-on-Avon.

Ionesco's *La Cantatrice Chauve* opens in Paris.

Don't Give Up Your Day Job

Critics in London generally agree that **Pablo Picasso** should definitely stick to painting after seeing his play *Desire Caught By The Tail* written during the Nazi occupation of Paris in 1941.

The Real King Of The Blues

Thailand's young 22-year old saxophonist king, **Bhumibol Adulyadej** could actually give up *his* day job as five of his songs hit the Thai pop charts and a royal medley of his songs including *Blue Night* are featured in *Michael Todd's Peep Show* on Broadway.

WHAT A YEAR IT WAS!

Dance

FAMOUS BIRTH
Debbie Allen

FAMOUS BIRTH

Debbie Allen

✳ Cecil Beaton designs the costumes and sets for the new ballet "Illuminations," score by Benjamin Britten and choreography by Frederick Ashton.

✳ New pieces premiere at the American Dance Festival including José Limon's "Concert," set to Bach fugues and preludes, and an untitled piece by Jane Dudley danced to music by Bartok.

✳ Frederick Ashton's "Les Patineurs" and Adolph Bolm's "Peter and the Wolf" kick off the ballet theatre season at New York's Center Theatre followed by Antony Tudor's "Judgment of Paris" and "La Fille Mal Gardee" and Jerome Robbins' "Fancy Free."

✳ Great Britain forms the English National Ballet.

✳ Martha Graham troupe first U.S. dance company to perform in Paris since World War II.

BALANCHINE

In a tribute to beaches and the young people who fill them **GEORGE BALANCHINE** premieres his **Jones Beach** ballet which begins with 36 dancers wearing colorful bathing suits.

Pas de deux romantique, Pas de deux from **Sylvia** and **Mazurka** from **A Life For The Tsar** are three new works choreographed by **GEORGE BALANCHINE** and presented by the New York City Ballet.

Maria Tallchief dances the title role beautifully to **GEORGE BALANCHINE'S** choreography and **MARC CHAGALL'S** magnificent set in **IGOR STRAVINSKY'S Firebird.** Stravinsky conducts the opening night performance of the New York City Ballet's production at City Center.

Jerome Robbins dances the title role in **GEORGE BALANCHINE'S** revival of his **Prodigal Son** for the New York City Ballet Company.

The 1920's **Charleston** grows in popularity.

Over 8,000 dancers guided by 36 callers show up in Santa Monica, California for the world's largest square dance jamboree.

Antony Tudor's New Ballet Nimbus Receives Mixed Reviews At Its Premiere Performance In New York.

Celebrating Its 10th Anniversary, The Ballet Theatre Opens Its Season With Les Sylphides.

Roland Petit's Les Ballets De Paris Performs La Croqueuse de Diamants In America For The First Time.

Britain's Sadler's Wells Ballet On Its First National Tour Of The United States Featuring Prima Ballerina **Margot Fonteyn** Breaks Box-Office Records During Its 3-Week Run At The Metropolitan Opera House Where They Perform Giselle, Dante Sonata and Don Quixote.

Passing

Famed Russian ballet dancer and choreographer **VASLAV NIJINSKY**, who danced with the Russian Imperial Ballet and Sergei Diaghilev's company, dies at age 60.

WHAT A YEAR IT WAS!

Classical Music

🎵 **Pablo Casals**, the world's finest cellist, comes out of retirement to play at the Bach Commemorative Festival in the village of Prades in the French Pyrenees celebrating the 200th anniversary of Bach's death.

🎵 **The San Diego Philharmonic Orchestra** is San Diego's first professional orchestra.

🎵 **12,600 people** attend the closing concert at the Berkshire Festival.

Machine Guns & Music Surrounded by heavy security, *YEHUDI MENUHIN* begins a 12-day benefit concert tour of Israel.

Sergei Prokofiev

PETER AND THE WOLF composer **SERGEI PROKOFIEV** announces his latest work for children is called GUARDING PEACE.

ELEANOR ROOSEVELT makes her musical debut as the narrator in Prokofiev's fable PETER AND THE WOLF.

Pulitzer Prize for Music

The Consul
Gian-Carlo Menotti

Gian-Carlo Menotti

Rounding Out The Corners

Gian-Carlo Menotti's opera <u>The Medium</u> gets its first theatre-in-the-round performance at Broadway's first panoramic theatre. His latest opera, <u>The Consul</u> receives critical acclaim and is called his most successful opera.

Feel Free To Throw A Tomato Or Two

Aaron Copland and **Gian-Carlo Menotti** tell a luncheon crowd that they shouldn't feel badly if they don't like modern compositions as "most modern music is very bad."

AN ANXIOUS MOMENT

LEONARD BERNSTEIN conducts his original composition *The Age Of Anxiety* at Carnegie Hall with the New York Philharmonic Symphony Orchestra.

WHAT A YEAR IT WAS!

14-Year Old **Anna Maria Alberghetti** Makes A Dazzling Debut At Carnegie Hall And Becomes An Instant Diva.

HITTING NEW HIGHS AND LOWS

28-Year Old Peruvian Singer **YMA SUMAC** Receives Top Critical Acclaim At Her Hollywood Bowl Debut Where Her Four-Octave Range Stuns The Audience.

He's All Washed Up Around Here

A blast of water from a fire hose in the wings calls visiting Met tenor **Eugene Conley's** attention to the fact that his sleeve is on fire as he is singing *Rigoletto* in Verona, Italy.

An enthusiastic performance of "The Marriage of Figaro" ends the New York City Opera's 13th season.

Ending On A Low Note

After 24 years tenor **Lauritz Melchior** sings his last note at the Metropolitan Opera House due to a dispute with new general manager **Rudolf Bing**.

Rise Stevens and **Lawrence Tibbett** star in the world radio premiere of Mussorgsky's musical folk-drama **Khovanchina** broadcast live from the Metropolitan Opera House.

Lots Of Dough, Ra, Me

Under **Rudolf Bing's** management, the Metropolitan Opera packs the house taking in a record $50,000 in box office receipts for the season's opening performance of *Don Carlo*.

ONE WOMAN'S POISON IS ANOTHER WOMAN'S DESSERT

20-year old **Roberta Peters** *makes her Metropolitan Opera debut as she takes over the female lead in Mozart's* Don Giovanni *when the lead soprano is struck down with food poisoning.*

The Metropolitan Opera presents a new Americanized high-spirited version of Strauss' **Fledermaus**, which is performed with technical brilliance and enormous energy.

WELL, EXCUUUSE MY BACK

American contralto **MARIAN ANDERSON** sings to 1,200 music lovers at London's Royal Albert Hall—some of whom are seated in the organ gallery behind the stage.

Under **Sir Thomas Beecham's** *leadership England's Royal Philharmonic Orchestra begins its first American tour by a British orchestra since 1912.*

TSK, TSK, TSK... *Calling the audience a bunch of savages, ill-tempered conductor* **Sir Thomas Beecham** *is furious because of inappropriate applause during a performance of* Ariadne auf Naxos *at the Edinburgh Music Festival.*

Clarinetist **ARTIE SHAW** moves out of the usual jazz joints and plays in a classical concert hall performing **A Concerto For Clarinet And Orchestra** by Norman Dello Joio.

Aaron Copland's new piece **Clarinet Concerto** is performed by **BENNY GOODMAN** and the NBC Symphony Orchestra.

WHAT A YEAR IT WAS!

The air is yours... **use it**

to keep your business trips on schedule

MODERN science has now made air travel one of the most reliable forms of winter transportation. Nowadays, it's seldom that a flight does not arrive on time; even in weather that makes surface travel long-delayed.

When you're planning your next business trip, ask your airline or travel agent to show you how reliably, quickly and economically you can make it by air.

United Aircraft
CORPORATION
EAST HARTFORD, CONNECTICUT

Makers of Pratt & Whitney Engines, Hamilton Standard Propellers, Chance Vought Aircraft and Sikorsky Helicopters for the U. S. Armed Forces and the Finest Airlines in the World.

Art

THREE MODERN ART MUSEUMS deliver a joint "Statement on Modern Art," declaring *"...It is a museum's duty to present the art that it considers good, even if it is not yet generally accepted... Contrary to those who attack the advanced artists as antisocial, we believe in his spiritual and social role."*

NEARLY FORTY ARTISTS send an open letter protesting the Metropolitan Museum's jury selection for a painting competition. **Willem de Kooning, Robert Motherwell, Mark Rothko** and **Jackson Pollock** are among those who refuse to submit works and declare *"The organization of the exhibition and the choice of the jurors...does not warrant any hope that a just proportion of advanced art will be included."* Exhibited artists include **Edward Hopper, Andrew Wyeth, Rico Lebrun** and **Max Beckmann**.

AN EDVARD MUNCH EXHIBIT travels from Boston's Institute of Contemporary Art to New York's Museum of Modern Art.

ST. LOUIS' CITY ART MUSEUM pays $130,000 for Rembrandt's "Portrait Of A Young Man."

SCIENTISTS AT HARVARD'S FOGG ART MUSEUM give the okay to open an ancient scroll thought to have part of the Old Testament including the tale of Noah's father.

NEW YORK'S WHITNEY MUSEUM mounts the most colossal **Edward Hopper** retrospective ever held.

FERNAND LÉGER is shown in London for the first time, at the Tate Gallery, and **Berthe Morisot** is given her first extensive show in the English capital.

And in his spare time...

Several years after saving the Western World, WINSTON CHURCHILL loses his amateur artist ranking as Hallmark reproduces some of Winnie's originals on several products including Christmas cards and calendars.

The U.S. Treasury Department disagrees with many art experts and concludes that a questionable picture owned by William Goetz is indeed an original **Van Gogh**.

Pablo Picasso receives the International Peace Prize for Arts from the Communist World Peace Congress.

WHAT A YEAR IT WAS!

Staten Island housecleaner **Julia Asmus**, who paints on used canvases, has a New York showing of her work.

Celebrating the oft-ignored woman artist, the 24th annual San Francisco exhibition of female artists displays works of art created by the fairer sex.

The only granny in the art world, **Grandma Moses** shows her paintings in Europe—Switzerland, France, Austria and the Netherlands—for the first time.

Andrew Wyeth is named to the National Institute of Arts and Letters

Joan Miró is commissioned to create a mural for Harvard

Diego Rivera is working on a new mural in Mexico's National Palace

Robert Motherwell

Gallery Exhibits

William Baziotes, Kootz, New York

Cecil Beaton, Hugo, New York

Alexander Calder, Galerie Maeght, Paris

Salvador Dali, Carstairs, New York

Edgar Degas, The Lefevre Gallery, London

Jean Dubuffet, Pierre Matisse, New York

Raoul Dufy, Frank Perls Gallery, Beverly Hills

Alberto Giacometti, Pierre Matisse, New York

Juan Gris, Buchholz Gallery, New York

Paul Klee, New Art Circle, New York

Rico Lebrun, Jepson Art Institute, Los Angeles

René Magritte, Van Diemen, New York

Laszlo Moholy-Nagy, Pinacotheca, New York

Grandma Moses, The American-British Art Gallery, New York

Robert Motherwell, Society of the Four Arts, Palm Beach

Georgia O'Keeffe, An American Place, New York

Jackson Pollock, Betty Parsons Gallery, New York

Man Ray, Frank Perls Gallery, Beverly Hills

Pierre-Auguste Renoir, Wildenstein, New York

Mark Tobey, Willard, New York

Toulouse-Lautrec, Kleeman, New York

Vincent Van Gogh, Chicago Art Institute, Chicago

Max Weber, Rosenberg Galleries, New York

"Rodin And His Heritage" is shown at New York's Buchholz Gallery, along with **Alexander Calder**, **Georges Braque** and **Henry Moore**.

Color lithographs by **Marc Chagall** inspired by "Arabian Nights" on view at the Cincinnati Museum.

- The little boy who stuck his finger in a dike and saved Holland is now immortalized as a bronze statue in the Dutch town of Haarlem.

- 1,000 old-timers over 60 display dioramas, dolls and other homemade trinkets at The Hobby Show For Older Persons.

- Resolutions are ratified in Paris to increase the presence of sculpture in government buildings.

- A comprehensive **Henri Matisse** retrospective commences in Nice, France.

- New York's National Academy of Design turns 125.

1950 PAINTINGS

Jackson Pollock	**Lavender Mist: Number 1, 1950**
Pablo Picasso	**Claude & Paloma At Play**
Andy Warhol	**Man**
Max Beckmann	**Columbine**
Joan Miró	**Characters In The Night**
Salvador Dali	**The Madonna Of Port-Lligat**

Salvador Dali

AUCTION HIGHLIGHTS

SOLD... to the lady in the pillbox hat

Raphael	*Peruzzi Madonna*	$ 27,000
Modigliani	*Reclining Nude*	$ 12,500
Degas	*Dancers*	$ 8,400
Kokoschka	*Tower Bridge, London*	$ 5,500
Goya	*Disparates* (etching)	$ 25

MUSEUM ACQUISITIONS

Brancusi	*Fish*	Museum of Modern Art
Cézanne	*Victor Choquet*	Columbus Gallery of Fine Art
Mondrian	*Color Squares In Oval*	Museum of Modern Art
Picasso	*Harlequin*	Museum of Modern Art
Rousseau	*Jungle*	Cleveland Museum
Titian	*Endymion*	The Barnes Foundation

At the 25th Venice Biennial *new and returning artists from 22 nations exhibit 4,000 pieces. France's* **Henri Matisse** *wins first prize, while American painter* **John Marin** *is given a one-man show. Works of popular artists* **Pablo Picasso, Georges Rouault, Marc Chagall** *and* **Maurice Utrillo** *hang in the French pavilion.*

The Carnegie Institute's annual exhibit is international for the first time since 1939. The Winners:

1st Prize	$2,000	**Jacques Villon**, France	The Thresher
2nd Prize	$1,000	**Lyonel Feininger**, USA	Houses By The River
3rd Prize	$800	**Priscilla Roberts**, USA	Self-Portrait

PASSING

German-born expressionist painter and printmaker **MAX BECKMANN**, known for his tortured figures, apocryphal triptychs and stunning self-portraits, dies at age 66. Beckmann spent the World War II years in Berlin before emigrating to the United States where he settled in St. Louis.

WHAT A YEAR IT WAS!

books

Across The River And Into The Trees
Ernest Hemingway

The Anatomy Of Villainy
Nigel Balchin

Another Pamela;
Or, Virtue Still Rewarded
Upton Sinclair

The Assyrian, And Other Stories
William Saroyan

The Ballad Of New York, New York,
And Other Poems
Christopher Morley

Bernard Baruch, Portrait Of A
Citizen
W.L. White

Betty Crocker's Picture Cook Book
Betty Crocker

Body And Mature Behaviour
Moshe Feldenkrais

Burning Bright, A Play In Story Form
John Steinbeck

Captain's Death Bed And
Other Essays
Virginia Woolf

The Cardinal
Henry Morton Robinson

Case History Of A Movie
Dore Schary

The Case Of The One-Eyed Witness
Erle Stanley Gardner

Cast A Cold Eye
Mary McCarthy

Childhood & Society
Erik Erikson

Coming Up For Air
George Orwell

Complete Poems
Carl Sandburg

Connie Mack's Baseball Book
Connie Mack

The Country Wife
Dorothy Van Doren

Dark Green, Bright Red
Gore Vidal

The Delicate Prey And Other Stories
Paul Bowles

The Disenchanted
Budd Schulberg

Dianetics
L. Ron Hubbard

The Federal Bureau
Of Investigation
Max Lowenthal

The Meaning Of Relativity
Albert Einstein

A Generation On Trial
Alistair Cooke

Goethe The Scientist
Rudolf Steiner

The Grand Alliance
Winston S. Churchill

Grass Is Singing
Doris Lessing

The Great Escape
Lt. Paul Brickhill

Helena
Evelyn Waugh

The Human Use Of Human Beings;
Cybernetics And Society
Norbert Wiener

If I Ran The Zoo
Dr. Seuss

James Joyce's Dublin
Patricia Hutchins

Joy Street
Frances Parkinson Keyes

Albert Einstein

PRIZES

NOBEL

Literature:
BERTRAND RUSSELL

PULITZER

Fiction:
A.B. GUTHRIE, JR.
The Way West

Poetry:
GWENDOLYN BROOKS
Annie Allen

History:
OLIVER W. LARKIN
Art And Life In America

National Reporting:
EDWIN O. GUTHMAN
Seattle Times

Local Reporting:
MEYER BERGER
New York Times

International Reporting:
EDMUND STEVENS
The Christian Science Monitor

Editorial Cartooning:
JAMES T. BERRYMAN
The Evening Star, Washington DC

Biography or Autobiography:
SAMUEL FLAGG BEMIS
John Quincy Adams And The Foundations Of American Foreign Policy

Kon-Tiki
   Thor Heyerdahl

The Legacy
   Nevil Shute

The Life Of Mahatma Gandhi
   Louis Fischer

The Little Princesses
   Marion Crawford

Local Color
   Truman Capote

Look Younger, Live Longer
   Gayelord Hauser

The Marx Brothers
   Kyle Crichton

The Martian Chronicles
   Ray Bradbury

The Maugham Reader
   W. Somerset Maugham

The Maverick Queen
   Zane Grey

Mister Jelly Roll
   Alan Lomax

The Parasites
   Daphne du Maurier

Pebble In The Sky
   Isaac Asimov

Paterson, Book III
   William Carlos Williams

The Prospect Before Us
   John Dos Passos

Psychoanalysis And Religion
   Erich Fromm

Reflections Of A Wondering Jew
   Morris Raphael Cohen

The Roman Spring Of Mrs. Stone
   Tennessee Williams

Roosevelt In Retrospect:
   A Profile In History
   John Gunther

Scenes From Provincial Life
   William Cooper

W. Somerset Maugham

The School For Wives
   André Gide

Scottsboro Boy
   **Hayward Patterson &
   Earl Conrad**

Selected Essays
   T.S. Eliot

They All Played Ragtime
   Rudi Blesh & Harriet Janis

The Third Man
   Graham Greene

The Thirteen Clocks
   James Thurber

A Town Like Alice
   Nevil Shute

The Town And The City
   Jack Kerouac

Vengeance Is Mine
   Mickey Spillane

The Wall
   John Hersey

The Wisdom Of The Sands
   Antoine de Saint-Exupery

World Enough And Time
   Robert Penn Warren

Famous Birth

Fran Lebowitz

Prophetic British author **George Orwell**, who depicts societies gone bad in *ANIMAL FARM* and *1984*, dies at age 46. Orwell named *1984* simply by reversing the last numbers of 1948, the year he wrote the novel.

•

TARZAN author **Edgar Rice Burroughs**, whose many books have been translated into a multitude of languages and have sold multi-millions worldwide, dies at age 74. His ape-man also garnered success in movies and comic strips, and Burroughs even named the town of Tarzana, California after his best-known creation.

•

Pulitzer Prize winning poet **Edna St. Vincent Millay** dies of a heart attack at age 58.

•

Scholar, author, editor, historian, literary critic and Pulitzer Prize winner for his biography on Benjamin Franklin, **Carl Van Doren** dies at age 64.

1950

books

Jack Kerouac writes the first draft of *ON THE ROAD*.

The Library of Congress turns 150.

A MURDER IS ANNOUNCED is the 50th novel written by AGATHA CHRISTIE.

Pocket Books sells its 300 millionth edition.

Thomas Mann, William Carlos Williams, Robert Penn Warren and Ogden Nash are elected to the National Institute of Arts and Letters. New honorary members include ANDRÉ GIDE and JAWAHARLAL NEHRU.

E.E. Cummings is given a $5,000 fellowship from the Academy of American Poets.

The Pulitzer Prize for poetry goes to GWENDOLYN BROOKS— the first Negro writer to receive the prestigious award.

NATIONAL BOOK AWARD
— FICTION —
Nelson Algren
"The Man With The Golden Arm"
— POETRY —
William Carlos Williams
"Paterson III" and "Selected Poems"

AMERICAN ACADEMY OF ARTS AND LETTERS
— HOWELLS MEDAL —
William Faulkner
— GOLD MEDAL —
H.L. Mencken

According to a poll of literary professionals, **The Faerie Queen, Don Quixote, Paradise Lost** and **Moby Dick** are some of the dullest classics ever written.

DISASTERS

An earthquake measuring over 8.6 on the Richter scale, the second highest in history, hits India, Tibet and Burma displacing 5 million people and devastating the land.

80 people die in the crash of a chartered airliner in South Wales making it the worst air crash in aviation history.

300,000 are homeless as a typhoon devastates the northern island of Hokkaido, Japan.

51 die in a deadly blast when a French weather ship strikes a World War II mine floating in the English Channel.

Multiple earthquakes kill 1,500 in Iran.

An estimated 10,000,000 people are displaced by the flooding Hwai river in the Anhwei province in China.

What began with merriment ends in disaster as 28 Brazilians are killed and over 4,500 are injured during Carnival in Rio de Janeiro.

The West Coast is hit by 70-mile an hour winds and snow in one of the severest blizzards in 50 years.

58 people perish when a Northwest airliner crashes into Lake Michigan outside of Milwaukee, making it the worst commercial airline crash in U.S. history.

Over 200 people are injured and 78 are killed when a Long Island railroad express train crashes into the back of a standing local in Richmond Hill, New York.

Over 30 commuters die and over 100 are injured when two Long Island railroad passenger trains have a head-on collision in Rockville Centre, New York.

41 women, most of whom are mental patients, are burned to death at Mercy Hospital in Davenport, Iowa as flames sweep through their ward.

A troop train crashes in Ohio killing 33 soldiers.

A military plane loaded with an A-Bomb plunges into a California trailer park killing 17 and injuring 60.

20 people die and 400 are injured in an explosion of ammunition barges in New Jersey.

The Truckee, Yuba and American rivers swell due to heavy rains melting the snow cap on the Sierras causing flood damage estimated at $25,000,000 in California and Nevada.

In the worst city traffic accident in U.S. history 33 die a fiery death and 40 are injured in Chicago when a gasoline truck collides with a trolley car during a driving rainstorm.

Topping the 1913 blizzards, record snow-storms sweep the eastern seaboard killing 250 people with Pittsburgh getting an unprecedented 23 inches of snow.

The American River flood leaves 1,000 people homeless near Laton and an estimated $100,000 worth of turkeys drown.

Fashion

*F*ashion guru **Christian Dior** sings the virtues of the "Guitar Look" for women – broad hips and bosom with a slender waist. If you don't naturally have this body, diet and exercise combined with the proper under-garments can help achieve it.

*F*or his contribution to the fashion industry, **Christian Dior** is awarded the French Legion of Honour.

Balenciaga shows a tweed suit with velvet collar, **Lanvin** spruces up a white dress with a smidgen of black, **Schiaparelli** presents whimsical pirate slacks and **Fath** offers a pleated blouse.

NO PEEKING

*P*aris designers create women's skirts a full three inches shorter than last year, with some of **Dior's** stopping a whopping 16 inches from the floor.

*E*vening dresses are cut nearly to the navel, showing a lot of décolletage, while diagonal cuts, checks and fuzzy fabrics are seen at most fashion houses.

The International Jewelry
Shows Off A Million Dollars I

This is the first time these fabulous jewels are displayed in Spain before their public showing.

These treasures by French, English, American and Spanish designers are among the gorgeous pieces that will adorn some lucky women throughout the world.

Expo In Barcelona, Spain
Dazzling Gems.

These marvelous diamonds once worn by royalty boast histories that go back through the centuries.

Rubies from Burma, sapphires from India, emeralds from South America – all these precious stones sparkle in hand-wrought settings, many of which were inspired by the Far East.

Classical styles in gold and platinum are among the finest creations of the world's greatest artisans.

1950

HOPALONG CASSIDY

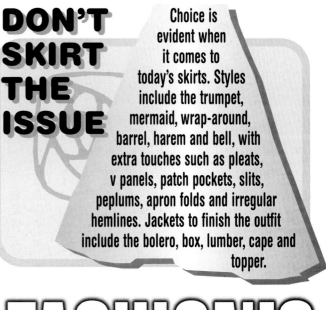

clothes are kids' favorite Western-wear.

Italian designers gain in popularity as Americans tire of the costly prices many French designers charge.

Edgar Bergen visits the House of Balmain in Paris to purchase a dress for new dummy Podine Puffington.

ALL THIS AND FRANKIE TOO!

Bobby-soxers are given a "toes up" by Dr. Carlo Scuderi, who believes the youngsters' choice of low-heeled and wide-toed shoes will result in improved foot fitness.

HUP, TWO, THREE, FOUR—

LOOKING GOOD FOR THE NEXT WAR

The Army's women are marching to a different tune as they begin wearing Hattie Carnegie designed uniforms. Standout features include gold buttons, handsome taupe color, spiffy hats and an overall feminine look.

DON'T SKIRT THE ISSUE

Choice is evident when it comes to today's skirts. Styles include the trumpet, mermaid, wrap-around, barrel, harem and bell, with extra touches such as pleats, v panels, patch pockets, slits, peplums, apron folds and irregular hemlines. Jackets to finish the outfit include the bolero, box, lumber, cape and topper.

FASHION'S GOING TO THE DOGS

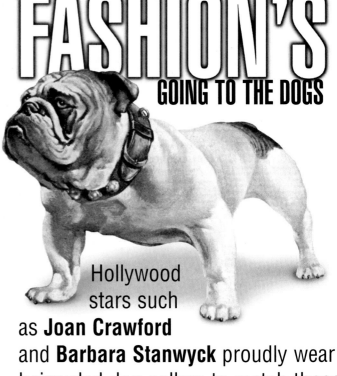

Hollywood stars such as **Joan Crawford** and **Barbara Stanwyck** proudly wear bejeweled dog collars to match those of their pups.

Colorful COORDINATION

Colors and materials of the year include orange, chiffon, taffeta, red, lace, crepe, violet, velvet, shantung, yellow, satin, georgette, grey, organdy, silk, green, linen, voile, black with white, wool and navy.

Retailer Harold Marcus sends **Neiman-Marcus** clothes and models to Australia to persuade those Down Under to buy Yankee-wear.

bare IS BETTER

Sleeveless and strapless dresses for day or evening show off your lovely arms, shoulders and back as does the popular halter dress.

Long gloves or unattached sleeves can change the look in an instant without covering up. Sleeveless or short sleeve coats complete the ensemble.

Concerning the weighty matter of weight, nearly all American women feel overweight while most men think women are underweight.

From New York to Paris and everywhere in between, the chemise remains a favorite with women of all sizes, contrasting form-fitting fashions made for a slimmer body.

hat trap

What man can resist the latest crop of ladies' hats? For those single women John-Frederics presents his oversized "Man Trap," certain to catch an extra look from that special somebody, while Lille Dache's "Flying Saucer" might turn an alien head or two.

Small or large, other styles sure to attract attention include the cloche, bicorne, tricorne, sailor, cocarde, pillbox, toque, skimmer, teacup and bonnet, with veils adding a touch of mystery.

Accessorize Accessorize,

come on everybody please accessorize

Big, big, big is your best choice.

Big faux jeweled pins on hats or sleeve cuffs, big artificial flowers for your hair or hat and big rhinestone earrings dangling by your curly locks improve casual and formal costumes.

An eye made of jewels worn in the third eye area is an innovative fashion accessory created by **Salvador Dali.**

Gloves, bows, ribbons and scarves are the small details that complete any outfit.

Shoe-be-dooby-do

One day your immaculate toes poke through your open toe shoes, the next day your toes are covered by a Turkish toe opera pump, embellished with lace, embroidery or buckles.

Strappy striplings look dainty but are strong enough to hold your foot in all day long.

Ankle-strap sandals, the wedge and a casual flat put your best foot forward in the day, with high-heels remaining the nighttime heel of choice.

486 MILLION PAIRS OF SHOES ARE MANUFACTURED IN AMERICA.

1950 ADVERTISEMENT

The Department of Agriculture joins the ranks of Paris and New York by having their own fashion show in Washington, DC. A rain poncho for children is among the practical do-it-yourself models, costing only $2.00.

An Orlon Fashion Show Displays The New Washable Man-Made Material.

The first National Beauty Salon Week is held during October.

Passings

One of the founders of the high-end Neiman-Marcus store, **Herbert Marcus** dies of a heart attack at age 72.

Ellis Gimbel, who, along with his father and brothers, helped make the Gimbel and Saks Fifth Avenue department stores household names, dies at 84. Chairman of the Board, Gimbel was known as much for his philanthropy as for being the first to put in store escalators.

Ellis Gimbel

hair today, gone tomorrow

Controversy rages over short versus long hair, with most stylists in the know opting to keep tresses trimmed.

Upswept locks remain popular along with pin curls, waves, bangs and ringlets.

Women continue their love affair with the gamin, pageboy and chignon styles.

152

WHAT A YEAR IT WAS!

1950

A STRIDE AHEAD IN FIT AND VALUE

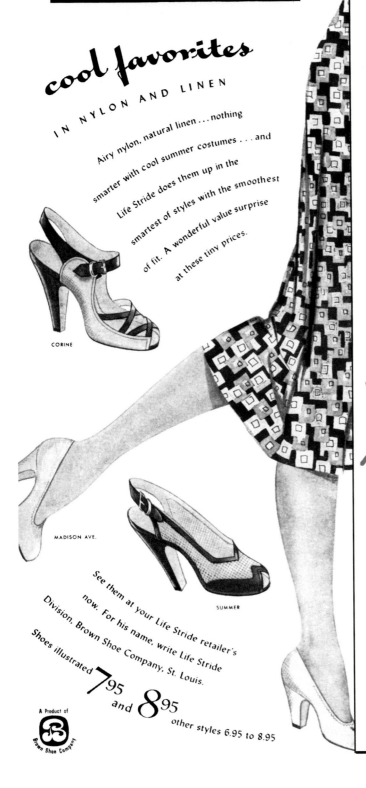

cool favorites

IN NYLON AND LINEN

Airy nylon, natural linen ... nothing smarter with cool summer costumes ... and Life Stride does them up in the smartest of styles with the smoothest of fit. A wonderful value surprise at these tiny prices.

CORINE

MADISON AVE.

SUMMER

See them at your Life Stride retailer's now. For his name, write Life Stride Division, Brown Shoe Company, St. Louis.

Shoes illustrated 7.95 and 8.95

other styles 6.95 to 8.95

A Product of
Brown Shoe Company

The eyes have it – and are the focal point of your lovely face.

FACE-ing FACTS

Doe-eyes are reminiscent of yesteryear, with a strong line around the eye and bright colors on the lids, such as green, blue, gold or marcasite.

Bow-shaped lips are most kissable in silky red, orange or pink.

153

What other coin machine gives you 20,000-to-1 ODDS?

THIS COIN MACHINE, strangely enough, sells life insurance. It is a familiar sight in airports all over the country where it offers 20,000-to-1 odds that you will complete your trip safely.

Machines like this, installed by one of the nation's leading life insurance companies, sell individual trip insurance at 25¢ for a $5,000 policy. Life insurance companies are known to be conservative-minded business organizations that base their policies on the law of averages. They do not gamble foolishly.

What better evidence could you seek that Flagships today are not only faster and finer but *safer* than ever before than this standing offer of 20,000-to-1 on every trip you take.

America's Leading Airline **AMERICAN AIRLINES** INC.

154

BEST DRESSED

WOMEN

Swanson

Gloria Swanson

Mrs. William Paley

Duchess of Windsor

Duchess of Windsor

Lynn Fontanne

Gertrude "Gussie" Moran

Margaret Chase Smith

Mrs. Hearst

Faye Emerson

Sloan Simpson O'Dwyer

Mrs. William Randolph Hearst, Jr.

Mrs. Leland Howard

MEN

General Dwight D. Eisenhower

Ezzard Charles

Leopold Stokowski

Flynn

Ralph Edwards

Errol Flynn

Barkley

Arthur Murray

Vice President Alben Barkley

Sammy Kaye

Henry J. Kaiser

Robert Montgomery

WORST DRESSED MEN

Prince Aly Khan

Gorgeous George

Alfred Gwynne Vanderbilt

Men's Corner

Much to the chagrin of Savile Row, tartan dinner jackets are being worn by young and old alike on both sides of the Atlantic. When King George VI begins wearing them, "Tailor and Cutter" magazine acquiesces, "His Majesty will bring dignity to the garment."

Sleex pants with zippers on the waistband, eliminating the need for a belt, are introduced.

For the well-dressed and well-heeled man, try **garter clasps** in **14-karat gold.**

WHAT A YEAR IT WAS!

elegant Man

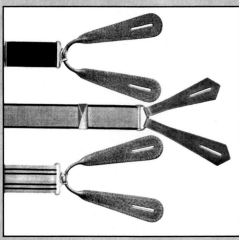

High-rise trousers held up with braces, a chambray shirt with an old-fashioned pin-point collar and a tweed jacket topped with a hat looks great at the office or a weekend party.

A contemporary wit has said that a man must be 45 before he can appreciate clothes, money or women. How neat but how inaccurate. The popularity of Hart Schaffner & Marx clothes with men of all ages is enough to disprove him on all three counts. For they are bought by those who evidently enjoy looking their best . . . who realize that good clothes are always an economy in the long run . . . and are willing to take the risk of being admired.

The gentleman above is wearing one of our famous Triple Test® suits . . . in the new Arrowhead pattern.

HART SCHAFFNER & MARX®

SPORTS

Joe DiMaggio Story

Joe DiMaggio, idol of millions of baseball fans all over the nation, signs a new contract for another year with the champion New York Yankees.

The contract is rumored to be in the neighborhood of $100,000.

Joe gets the green light from George Weiss, General Manager of the great American League team.

If that number is correct, it means he has earned over $500,000 in his diamond career.

WHAT A YEAR IT WAS!

159

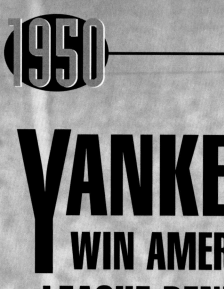

YANKEES

WIN AMERICAN LEAGUE PENNANT AND TAKE THEIR 13TH WORLD SERIES— BEATING THE PHILS IN A FOUR GAME SWEEP

Excited fans show up at Yankee Stadium.

Casey Stengel *(left)* has a friendly little chat with Philadelphia's Eddie Sawyer.

WHAT A YEAR IT WAS!

THE PITCH

IT'S A STRIKE

AND IT'S LUCKY 13 FOR THE NEW YORK CHAMPS

1950 Baseball

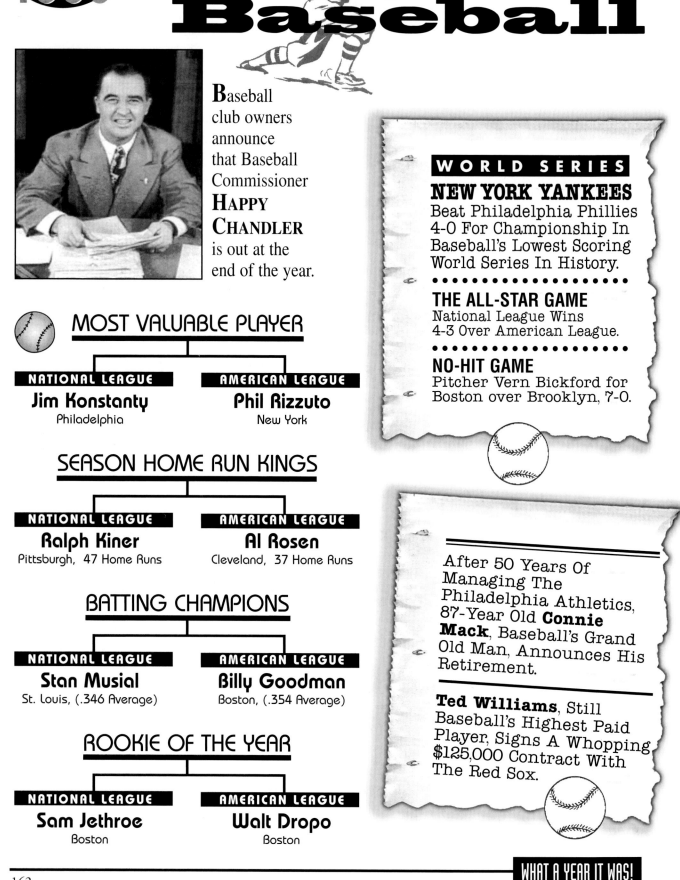

Baseball club owners announce that Baseball Commissioner **HAPPY CHANDLER** is out at the end of the year.

MOST VALUABLE PLAYER

NATIONAL LEAGUE	AMERICAN LEAGUE
Jim Konstanty	**Phil Rizzuto**
Philadelphia	New York

SEASON HOME RUN KINGS

NATIONAL LEAGUE	AMERICAN LEAGUE
Ralph Kiner	**Al Rosen**
Pittsburgh, 47 Home Runs	Cleveland, 37 Home Runs

BATTING CHAMPIONS

NATIONAL LEAGUE	AMERICAN LEAGUE
Stan Musial	**Billy Goodman**
St. Louis, (.346 Average)	Boston, (.354 Average)

ROOKIE OF THE YEAR

NATIONAL LEAGUE	AMERICAN LEAGUE
Sam Jethroe	**Walt Dropo**
Boston	Boston

WORLD SERIES
NEW YORK YANKEES
Beat Philadelphia Phillies 4-0 For Championship In Baseball's Lowest Scoring World Series In History.
• • • • • • • • • • • • • • • • •
THE ALL-STAR GAME
National League Wins 4-3 Over American League.
• • • • • • • • • • • • • • • • •
NO-HIT GAME
Pitcher Vern Bickford for Boston over Brooklyn, 7-0.

After 50 Years Of Managing The Philadelphia Athletics, 87-Year Old **Connie Mack**, Baseball's Grand Old Man, Announces His Retirement.

Ted Williams, Still Baseball's Highest Paid Player, Signs A Whopping $125,000 Contract With The Red Sox.

Baseball

- Brooklyn's First Baseman **Gil Hodges** Becomes The Fourth Man In Baseball History To Hit Four Home Runs In A Game.

- The Negro American League Hires White Players For The First Time.

- New York Yankees Slugger **Joe DiMaggio** Records Seven Episodes Of His *Joe DiMaggio Show* – A Saturday Morning CBS Radio Program For Children.

- Pitcher **Curt Simmons** Of The Philadelphia Phillies Is The First Major League Player Drafted For The Korean War.

- Called The "Fanciest Fielding First Baseman" Ever, Fort Lauderdale Gives **Dorothy Kamenshek** A Contract In Preparation Of Players Being Drafted For The Korean Conflict.

- **Branch Rickey** Chosen Vice President And General Manager Of The Pittsburgh Pirates.

The New Redhead On The Block

Sportscaster "Old Redhead" Red Barber Turns Up At The Brooklyn Dodgers Spring Training Camp In Florida To Celebrate His 16th Year Of Big-League Baseball Broadcasting, 20 Years Of Sports Announcing And An 11-Year Association With The Dodgers And Begins Breaking In A Youngster By The Name Of **Vin Scully** To Join The Dodgers Broadcasting Staff.

WALTER O'MALLEY

Becomes New President And Chief Stockholder Of The Brooklyn Dodgers.

New York's WNEW Radio Station Boasts The Youngest Sports Commentator In The World — 9-Year Old Charlie Hankinson.

ST. LOUIS CARDINALS
Beat The
PITTSBURGH PIRATES
4-2
In Baseball's First Nighttime Opener.

WHO YOU GONNA KILL
IF YOU DON'T LIKE THE CALL?

The Brooklyn Dodgers Use A New Electronic "Umpire" At Their Spring Training Camp Which Automatically Indicates Whether A Baseball Is A Strike Or A Ball.

FOOTBALL

Oklahoma Sooners

Extend Their Unbeaten Streak To 31 Winding Up #1 On Football's Hit Parade.

Led by quarterback Bob Arnold, the Sooners go through the season unbeaten and untied.

Arnold, halfback Billy Vessells and fullback Leon Heath make a touchdown.

The fans go wild!

164

Football

NATIONAL FOOTBALL LEAGUE CHAMPIONS

CLEVELAND BROWNS edge LOS ANGELES RAMS 30-28 for PRO TITLE

NAVY DEFEATS ARMY 12-2

Rose Bowl

OHIO STATE Beats CALIFORNIA 17-14

HEISMAN TROPHY

VIC JANOWICZ OHIO STATE

NATIONAL COLLEGE FOOTBALL CHAMPION

OKLAHOMA

NUMBER ONE DRAFT CHOICE

LEON HART of Notre Dame to Detroit

COLLEGE FOOTBALL COACH OF THE YEAR
Charlie Caldwell
(Princeton)

Notre Dame

University Stadium Admits Women In Its Press Box For The First Time But They Are Western Union Operators Sending The Newsmen's Copy.

BAKER BOWL,
Philadelphia's Historic Landmark Which Opened In April 1887, And Home To The Philadelphia Phillies, Is Demolished

San Francisco
49ers
JOIN THE NFL.

The National Football League And All-America Football Conference Merge.

WESTMINSTER KENNEL CLUB
Walsing Winning Trick of Edgerstoune, Scottish Terrier

DOG SHOW
WINNERS
MORRIS AND ESSEX SHOW
CHAMPION CLANCY, *Irish Setter*

WHAT A YEAR IT WAS!

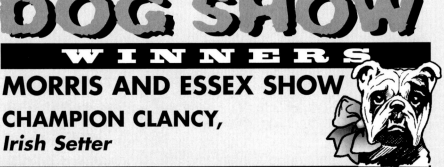

BASKETBALL

CCNY'S BEAVERS

win the National Invitation Tournament and the National Collegiate.

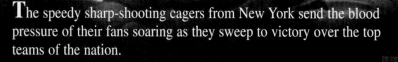

The speedy sharp-shooting cagers from New York send the blood pressure of their fans soaring as they sweep to victory over the top teams of the nation.

Hitting a jackpot unprecedented in basketball this year will long be remembered by coach Nate Holman and his eager Beavers from CCNY.

WHAT A YEAR IT WAS!

BASKETBALL

NBA CHAMPIONSHIP
MINNEAPOLIS LAKERS BEAT SYRACUSE, 4-2

NCAA & NIT CHAMPIONS
CCNY BEATS BRADLEY
NCAA : 71-68 | NIT : 69-61

NCAA MOST VALUABLE PLAYER
IRWIN DAMBROT — CCNY —

NBA SCORING LEADER
GEORGE MIKAN, MINNEAPOLIS 1,865 POINTS

WORLD BASKETBALL CHAMPIONS ARGENTINA

The Boston Celtics Draft *all-star* **CHARLES COOPER** Making Him The NBA's **First Negro Player.**

NIT MOST VALUABLE PLAYER
ED WARNER, CCNY

ROSS TROPHY
LEADING SCORER
Ted Lindsay, Detroit

VEZINA TROPHY
OUTSTANDING GOALIE
Bill Durnan, *Montreal*

STANLEY CUP CHAMPIONS
Detroit over NY Rangers, **4-3**

LADY BYNG MEMORIAL TROPHY
MOST GENTLEMANLY PLAYER
EDGAR LAPRADE, N.Y. Rangers

CALDER MEMORIAL TROPHY
ROOKIE OF THE YEAR
Jack Gelineau, Boston

HART MEMORIAL TROPHY (MVP)
Chuck Rayner, N.Y. Rangers

SOCCER
WORLD CUP
URUGUAY OVER **BRAZIL, 2-1**

CYCLING
Switzerland's **Ferdinand Kubler** Wins The Tour de France.

1950

BOXING

NEW YORK BOXER SUGAR RAY ROBINSON MAKES HIS EUROPEAN BOXING DEBUT

Following his Christmas Day knockout of Hans Stretz of Frankfurt, Germany, the Welterweight Champ strikes a sharp left jab to his opponent, France's Jean Stock, in a 10-round non-title bout.

Sugar Ray's blows to the body take the Frenchman to the floor for the second time *(left)* but he comes back for more *(below)*.

Dazed by the fury of his opponent's attack, Stock manages to get up on the count of seven.

WHAT A YEAR IT WAS!

Down again for the third time at two minutes of the second round, again the referee starts his count and again the plucky Frenchman manages to stagger to his feet.

Deciding his man has had enough, his manager throws in the towel.

For Sugar Ray Robinson his European debut is a huge and speedy success.

WHAT A YEAR IT WAS!

169

1950

EZZARD CHARLES BEATS JOE LOUIS FOR HEAVYWEIGHT BOXING TITLE

BOXING
WORLD TITLES

HEAVYWEIGHT
Joe Louis Fails In His Attempt To Win Back The Title And
Ezzard Charles Remains The Champ.

MIDDLEWEIGHT
Jake LaMotta

WELTERWEIGHT
Sugar Ray Robinson

FEATHERWEIGHT
Sandy Saddler

LIGHTWEIGHT
Ike Williams

LIGHT HEAVYWEIGHT
Joey Maxim

1947's Rookie of the Year, **Lavern Roach**, dies after being knocked out by Georgie Small in a New York comeback bout.

AP ATHLETE OF THE YEAR
baseball **Jim Konstanty**   *golf* **Babe Didrikson Zaharias**

GREATEST 20th Century ATHLETES
male **Jim Thorpe**   *female* **Babe Didrikson Zaharias**

Julius Erving

Famous Births

Mark Spitz

PASSING

Hall of Fame record-setting pitcher **Grover Cleveland Alexander**, who played for Chicago, St. Louis and Philadelphia during his long baseball career, dies at age 63.

WHAT A YEAR IT WAS!

GOLF

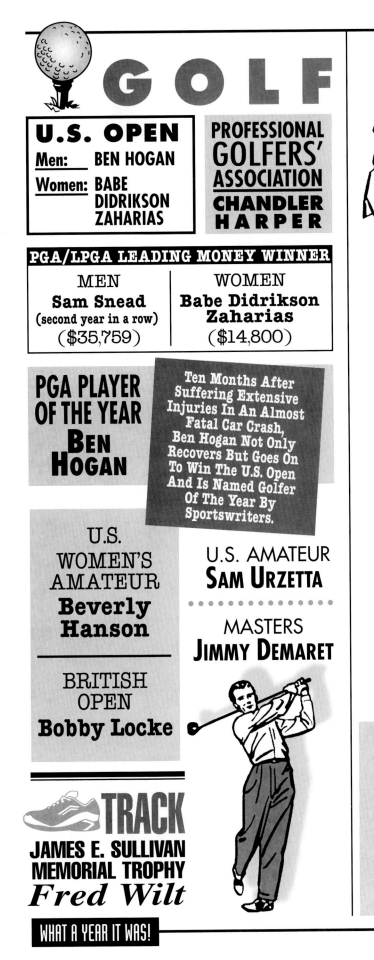

U.S. OPEN
Men: BEN HOGAN

Women: BABE DIDRIKSON ZAHARIAS

PROFESSIONAL GOLFERS' ASSOCIATION
CHANDLER HARPER

PGA/LPGA LEADING MONEY WINNER

MEN	WOMEN
Sam Snead (second year in a row) ($35,759)	**Babe Didrikson Zaharias** ($14,800)

PGA PLAYER OF THE YEAR
BEN HOGAN

Ten Months After Suffering Extensive Injuries In An Almost Fatal Car Crash, Ben Hogan Not Only Recovers But Goes On To Win The U.S. Open And Is Named Golfer Of The Year By Sportswriters.

U.S. WOMEN'S AMATEUR
Beverly Hanson

U.S. AMATEUR
SAM URZETTA

MASTERS
JIMMY DEMARET

BRITISH OPEN
Bobby Locke

TRACK

JAMES E. SULLIVAN MEMORIAL TROPHY
Fred Wilt

WHAT A YEAR IT WAS!

tennis

U.S. OPEN
— MEN —
Arthur Larsen over Herbert Flam

— WOMEN —
Margaret Osborne du Pont over Doris Hart

WIMBLEDON
— MEN —
Budge Patty* over Frank Sedgman

— WOMEN —
Louise Brough over Margaret Osborne du Pont

As a footnote to his Wimbledon win, Budge Patty reveals that he never could have won if he hadn't given up smoking.

DAVIS CUP
Australia over U.S., 4-1

With her entry in the United States Lawn Tennis Association, 22-year old New Yorker ALTHEA GIBSON becomes first Negro to compete in the United States tennis championships held at the West Side Tennis Club in Forest Hills, N.Y.

they're off!

That cry brings cheers from racing fans.

First in the Preakness, second in the Kentucky Derby, and winner of the Wood Memorial, three-year old "Hill Prince" is named Horse of the Year.

KENTUCKY DERBY

Middleground
ridden by
William Boland

PREAKNESS

Hill Prince
ridden by
Eddie Arcaro

Thrills, Chills And Spills At England's Grand National Steeplechase.

Many horses start this grueling test of man and mount but only a few get to finish.

Victory is in the balance until the very last jump. And we have a winner – the last horse still standing.

BELMONT STAKES

Middleground
ridden by
William Boland

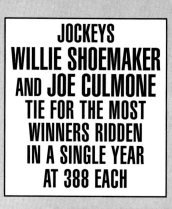

JOCKEYS WILLIE SHOEMAKER AND JOE CULMONE TIE FOR THE MOST WINNERS RIDDEN IN A SINGLE YEAR AT 388 EACH

WHAT A YEAR IT WAS!

BOWLING

The American Bowling Congress Removes Rule Restricting Membership To White Males And The Women's International Congress Removes Racial Clause From Its Membership Requirements.

AMERICAN BOWLING CONGRESS TOURNAMENT

Frank Santore Is All Events Winner Knocking Down 1,981 Pins

WOMEN'S INTERNATIONAL BOWLING CONGRESS

Mrs. Marion Ladewig All Events Winner

WORLD MATCH GAME CHAMPIONS

Ed Easter and Eddie Lubanski

SPORTS WRITERS AND BROADCASTERS VOTE ON THE TOP ATHLETES OF THE HALF CENTURY
(An AP Poll)

JACK DEMPSEY	Boxing
GEORGE MIKAN	Basketball
MAN O'WAR	Thoroughbred Racing
JESSIE OWENS	Track & Field
BABE RUTH	Baseball
JIM THORPE	Football
BILL TILDEN	Tennis
JOHNNY WEISSMULLER	Swimming

AUTO RACING

LE MANS
LOUIS ROSIER & JEAN-LOUIS ROSIER

WINSTON CUP CHAMPION
BILL REXFORD

INDIANAPOLIS 500
On Memorial Day With 150,000 Spectators Watching, Johnny Parsons Rides His Kurtis-Kraft Wynns Special At A Record Speed Of 124 m.p.h. Winning The Speedway Classic.

BILLIARDS

THREE-CUSHION CHAMP:
Willie Hoppe

WORLD POCKET-BILLIARD CROWN:
Willie Mosconi

FIGURE SKATING

The Women's World Figure Skating Champion Is Aja Vrzanova Of Czechoslovakia.

SWIMMING

Diving In The Water At Can Gris Nez, France, 24-Year Old Californian Florence Chadwick Swims The English Channel Reaching The Cliffs Of Dover In A Record 13 Hours, 23 Minutes.

CHESS

WORLD CHAMPION MIKHAIL BOTVINNIK, USSR

U.S. CHAMPION HERMAN STEINER

WHAT A YEAR IT WAS!

173

1950 WAS A GREAT YEAR, BUT...

THE BEST IS YET TO COME!